Give Up Worry Forever

SIMPLE STRATEGIES TO BRING PEACE AND ORDER TO YOUR LIFE

by
Dr. Robb Daniels Thompson

Harrison House
Tulsa, Oklahoma

09 08 07 06 05   10 9 8 7 6 5 4 3 2 1

Give Up Worry Forever:
Simple Strategies to Bring Peace and Order to Your Life
ISBN 1-57794-726-6
Copyright © 2005 by Robb Thompson
P. O. Box 558009
Chicago, Illinois 60655

Published by Harrison House, Inc.
P.O. Box 35035
Tulsa, Oklahoma 74153

Dedication

I want to dedicate this book
to all of those whose lives have been
controlled by panic and worry.

May the words on these pages
inspire you to reach for
the hand of freedom which God offers.
It is to you that I dedicate these words.

Table of Contents

Preface

Do you realize how much worrying you really do? Have you ever thought about what it would take in order for you to become worry-free? Never to worry again? I made my mind up some time ago that I didn't want to worry. I didn't want to be tied in knots when I dealt with the issues of life. That motivated me to study what causes us to worry, how it affects us, how we can avoid it, how we can get rid of it—and how we can stay rid of worry forever.

This book is a compilation of messages I have given through the years that describes what I have learned from studying and abiding in God's Word so that I could overcome worry, fear, anxiety, terror, and even panic attacks. Because I have personally been attacked by each of these and have had to overcome them—and because I know the devil never stops trying to scare us out of our faith in God, no matter how spiritually mature we are—I want to pass on to you what I have discovered in seeking His truth for the answers to my problems. I can tell you this without doubt or reservation: God's Word works!

I have also recorded a CD of Scriptures that I have studied, meditated, prayed, and confessed over myself and others through the years. God has used these verses to expose and expel the worries in my life and other people's lives so effectively that I want you to have them also. We have included this CD in this book for you to use. Listen to it. Memorize the Scriptures. Play it over and over until you have the Word of God so deeply embedded in your heart that no worry can ever take hold of you again.

Life on planet earth is hard enough without worrying our way through it! Jesus came that we might have abundant life (see John 10:10), and I don't think that includes wringing our hands over every issue and challenge we face! It is my prayer that this book will help you to recognize how worry captures your mind and affects your life, and that it will give you the wisdom and the tools to get free and stay free of it. There is nothing like going to sleep each night at peace with God and all that He is doing in your life. You can *Give Up Worry Forever!*

1

What Is Worry?

If you study the origin of the English word "worry," you will find that it means, "to strangle."[1] Worry will put its icy hand around your throat and begin to strangle you. It tries to destroy every part of your life. Worry also does this repeatedly. It keeps coming at you. It is an assailant that violently and aggressively attacks you over and over again, trying to choke the life and joy of God out of you. Here is Webster's definition, which I thought was very interesting.

> 1 a) to harass or treat roughly with or as with continual biting or tearing with the teeth [a dog worrying a bone]... 2 to annoy, bother, harass, vex, etc. 3 to cause to feel troubled or uneasy; make anxious; distress...something that causes anxiety.[2]

Have you ever watched a dog chew a bone? The animal is absolutely obsessed with getting every piece of meat off that bone, and then it will gnaw and gnaw at the bone itself, hour after hour, day after day. That is a perfect picture of how we worry over something in our lives. We are obsessed with it, covering every aspect, analyzing every possible scenario of doom and gloom, and too often making mountains out of molehills.

Worry is a mental condition that affects every other part of your being. It afflicts you with mental distress and agitation. Some synonyms of the word "worry" are to annoy, harass, vex, bother, fret, torment, distress. In most cases, the thing we're worried about has not happened and probably will never happen unless we worry our way into it. Still we are plagued and pestered by that worrying thought—and it is annoying!

Worry is destructive, causing mental disorders, physical distress, and even sickness. No matter how you look at it, worry is not a good thing.

WITNESS OR WORRY?

It is really important that we make a distinction between worry and having a witness from the Spirit that something is wrong. When the Holy Spirit gives us a witness that something is not right, that is not our cue to worry. That is our cue to pray, to get in God's Word, and to listen to the Holy Spirit so we know what we should be believing and praying according to God's Word. Then we won't worry because we will know it is in God's hands.

For example, I might get a witness in my spirit that something is wrong with one of my children. When that happens, I have to listen to my Comforter and Teacher. Then I can fight off my flesh and my natural mind because they want me to worry until I get into total fear. The moment I perceive in my spirit that something is not right, I have to begin praying in the Spirit and get God's Word on the situation. Then I can pray and stand in faith instead of falling into worry and fear. Worry is not going to help my child, but faith will move mountains for him.

FAITH OR WORRY?

Faith is the opposite of worry. When we have faith in God, we may still feel some uneasiness because we live in death-doomed flesh; but we are not worried in our hearts and minds.

This is the miracle of being a child of the Most High God. We can live in a world dominated by Satan and fear, we can be faced with all kinds of obstacles and catastrophe, and our flesh may react to these things in a negative or fearful manner. However, we can choose not to worry because in our hearts and minds we know the truth which keeps us free: God is in control, and He is our heavenly Father who loves us.

There is no other truth in the universe that can so transform you like the truth that God is your father and He loves you with an everlasting, all-forgiving love. When you truly grasp this infinite and unfathomable truth, this amazing grace that is yours, no matter what you are facing in life you can walk in faith in your God instead of worrying.

Worry Is Defeated by God's Love

No matter how you look at worry, no matter how it comes to you—through a thought, a nightmare, seeing something on television or a movie, hearing a story from a friend, or being faced with a real challenge in life—worry is always defeated in the face of God's love for you. When you understand, accept, and fully receive His unconditional love for you, most of what has worried you will float right out of your mind and heart. And that which does not immediately leave will eventually be driven away by renewing your mind with God's Word. Worry simply cannot stay in the same place with God's powerful love!

As you read through the rest of this book, you will gain a tremendous understanding of how worry comes into your life and how you can defeat it, avoid it, and be free of it. It is important for you to know these things. We can't defeat an enemy we don't acknowledge or understand, and we need to know how he is gaining entrance to our lives. That's why it is vital for you to get brutally honest with yourself about what bothers you.

You see, God is just waiting for you to come to Him about the stuff that really bugs you. In some cases, He is probably dealing with you about certain issues in your life that worry you. But because they make you uncomfortable and may even frighten you, you have turned away from Him again and again. It's time to stop pushing the Holy Spirit away and deal with it! You would not have picked up this book if He did not want you to face and overcome what is really worrying you.

Because I have had to deal with the worst kind of worrying there is, including panic attacks, I have full confidence in telling you that you are going to be so much better for facing, fighting, and defeating your worries and fears. Not only that, but you will not be facing them alone. You have the Father, Jesus, and the Holy Spirit right there with you. You have your church family and friends to help you. And you have God's Word to stand on. This is all part of God's love for you. His love for you is the truth that will set you free.

What is worry? Worry is the adversary that you are well on your way to defeating forever!

2

Four Causes of Worry

In my study of worry and my own experience with it over the years, I have discovered four things that will cause worry. When you understand the cause of something, you can then take steps to stop it. Once you locate the door through which worry is coming into your life, you can shut that door with God's Word and the power of His Spirit.

1. Taking authority over or responsibility for something that God has not given us.

Worry is caused by attempting to take authority over or responsibility for something that is none of our business. In 1 Thessalonians 4:11 NLT the Bible tells us, "You study to be quiet. You mind your own business and you do your own thing as you have been commanded to do." The original sin in the Garden of Eden happened because the woman stepped into a place of authority that God had not given to her.

> Now the serpent was more subtle than any beast of the field which the LORD God had made. And he said unto the woman, Yea, hath God said, Ye shall not eat of every tree of the garden?
>
> And the woman said unto the serpent, We may eat of the fruit of the trees of the garden:
>
> But of the fruit of the tree which is in the midst of the garden, God hath said, Ye shall not eat of it, neither shall ye touch it, lest ye die.

And the serpent said unto the woman, Ye shall not surely die:

For God doth know that in the day ye eat thereof, then your eyes shall be opened, and ye shall be as gods, knowing good and evil.

And when the woman saw that the tree was good for food, and that it was pleasant to the eyes, and a tree to be desired to make one wise, she took of the fruit thereof, and did eat, and gave also unto her husband with her; and he did eat.

And the eyes of them both were opened, and they knew that they were naked; and they sewed fig leaves together, and made themselves aprons.

GENESIS 3:1-7

In Genesis 3:3, the woman answered the devil incorrectly. She did not speak God's Word, but instead she spoke a twisted truth. Then she took the fruit and ate it. But notice that nothing happened. It wasn't until after she gave the fruit to her husband and he ate that their eyes were opened, they knew they were naked, and they had lost the Garden.

Why didn't the woman feel naked and guilty after she ate the fruit? Because her husband was the one in authority over the Garden. He was responsible and had the chance to change history, but he didn't. Instead, he ate of the fruit and brought sin to all human beings. But it all started to go wrong when the woman stepped into a place of authority that was not hers.

The Bible does not give us a clear understanding that God ever spoke to Eve or that she ever heard anything God said when He commanded Adam to keep and guard the Garden. It's very possible that Eve only knew what Adam told her. Whether or not Adam correctly instructed Eve in God's Word, we know that what Eve said to the serpent was not what God had said to Adam. She was speaking and acting on twisted truth. She didn't know God's Word, and because she did not know God's Word, she stepped into Adam's authority, gave him the fruit, and set in motion the fall of mankind.

One area where women are especially vulnerable is deception. That's why I tell the ladies of our church never to act upon a twisted truth. Whatever you believe should stand true all the way from Genesis to Revelation. Don't pick out some small little thing to justify something you want to do or you think sounds right and then base your entire life on it. Never do that! Believing and acting on a twisted truth can destroy you and bring down everything and everyone around you.

Men can be just as prone to step into authority that is not theirs, however. In our church I do not attempt to take authority over other people's responsibilities. I will not come into one of our employee's offices, put my feet up on their desk, act like their office is my office, and tell them how to do their job. I sit across the desk from them and respect the authority that I have given them to do what God has called them to do. I won't do it because they have a God-given seat of authority and responsibility; and if I violate that, I violate God's Word. Trusting God to lead them and guide them keeps me from worrying.

The same principle holds for the district pastors. I will not take authority in their districts. I will ask them about their productivity and how things are going, but I will not take the authority that is theirs. Why? That's their responsibility and their sphere of authority. If they are not faithful to do with integrity what God has called them to do or what I have instructed them to do, then I do have the authority to let them go. But I don't have the authority to do their job for them. When I remember this, I don't worry. I trust God to lead others in their sphere of authority.

This cause of worry happens in everyday situations as well. We all have pet peeves that can cause us worry and agitation, making us want to step in where we don't belong. Many people who know me understand that I tend to want to step in and interfere when it comes to moms and little kids in minivans.

Often the moms are distracted by the kids, who tend to make noise and get out of their car seats. And when I see a minivan on the road, I have visions of things growing between the seats because of the food that gets stuffed there. This is probably not as big a problem as I imagine it to be, but when I see a minivan, it is all I can do not to stop my car, flag it down, and become the local minivan inspector.

I would get in really big trouble if I started doing that because I'm not the authority in that minivan. More than that, I would be experiencing a lot of worry and agitation that could be avoided if I simply accepted the fact that that minivan is not my responsibility and I trusted God to take care of that situation.

The number one cause of worry is taking authority for things that are not our responsibility. We must learn to let go and trust God to take care of something. We must also learn to let go and trust God to work through the people He has set in authority over a situation. If I put someone in charge of a project in the church, and God has told me that is the person for the job, then I need to trust God and that person to get it done. You sleep a lot better when you don't worry about someone else's business.

2. Relinquishing the authority or responsibility God has given us.

It is true that we should not take the authority and responsibility that aren't ours, but the opposite is also true. We should never relinquish our God-given authority and responsibility. Let's go back to the Garden of Eden again.

> *Toward evening, they heard the Lord walking about in the garden, so they hid themselves from Him among the trees.*
> *And the Lord God said to Adam, "Where are you, Adam, where are you?"*
> *He replied, "I heard You so I hid. I was afraid because I was naked.*

And He said, "Who told you that you were naked? Have you
eaten of the fruit that I commanded you not to eat?"
"Yes," Adam admitted, "but it was the woman You gave me...."
GENESIS 3:8-12 NLT

In verse 12 Adam tries to lay the blame on the woman God
had given him, but notice that God didn't talk to Eve. He talked
to Adam. He said, "Where are you, Adam?" God had given
authority over the Garden to Adam, not Eve, so Adam was the
one He went looking for when things weren't right.

Later God said to Adam, "Because you listened to your wife
and ate the fruit that I told you not to eat, I have placed a curse
on the ground. All your life you will struggle to scratch a living
from it" (Genesis 3:17 NLT). God said, "Because you listened to
your wife." Here is the number two cause of worry: relinquishing your God-given authority and responsibility.

I believe Adam relinquished his authority in order to have
a counterfeit harmony with his wife. Many husbands do this
and it never comes to any good in a marriage and family. When
the husband continually relinquishes his authority in the home
just to have a moment's peace, he will begin to move
backwards, against God's Word. Instead of making life easier,
everything will get harder and harder. The same curse that
came upon Adam comes upon men who relinquish their God-
given authority and responsibility: they struggle harder and
harder to do what they are called to do. And this is why it
causes tremendous worry.

All your life you will sweat to produce food, until your dying
day, then you'll return to the ground from which you came. For you
were made from the dust and to the dust you will then return.
GENESIS 3:19

The consequence of relinquishing the authority and responsibility God gave Adam was that he struggled all the days of his life—because he did what his wife told him to do and did not do what God called him to do. As a result, the human race has been worrying about making a living ever since!

3. Not doing the assignment God has given us and pointing to others who aren't doing their assignment.

When we are not fulfilling our assignments, we are usually accusing others of not fulfilling theirs, usually pointing toward somebody who's not doing what we think they're supposed to do. We try to take the guilt and conviction we are under and put it on someone else.

That's exactly what Adam did when he didn't fulfill his assignment in the Garden. God had commanded him to cultivate it and to guard it. His job was to keep the serpent out. Not only did he allow the serpent in, but he also allowed it to carry on a conversation with his wife. After the fall, when God came to talk to Adam, he turned around and blamed it on the woman! That's the blame game.

Peter did this too. When Jesus confronted him about his calling to feed the sheep in John, chapter 21, Peter turned to Jesus and said, "What about John? What's John supposed to do?" You remember the story. Before the crucifixion Peter had denied Jesus three times. After the resurrection, Jesus came to Peter and asked him three times, "Peter, do you love Me?"

Peter said, "Lord, You know I love You."

Jesus said, "Then, feed My sheep." Peter had denied the Lord three times and three times Jesus reaffirmed Peter's call. The interesting part is that Peter now begins to change—and not for the better! You can go from guilt to arrogance in just a second if you are not watching your heart attitude. Because Jesus had reaffirmed Peter, Peter was feeling really good about himself. But instead of being grateful for being forgiven and reinstated, instead of being recharged to go out and do what God had called him to do, Peter proudly pointed his finger at John and said, "What about him?"

It's a funny thing about being forgiven and reaffirmed. Instead of repenting and changing, some people don't want to change. They don't really care that they are forgiven. They just want to be back on top so they can continue doing what they've always been doing. They believe that since they have favor again, they can go back to their old habits. This takes them from guilt to arrogance and pride—and pride always brings you down.

Linda gave me the perfect analogy for this. She had read a book about what happens to a baby when it is breach. In most cases, the doctor can manipulate the child into its proper birth position, turning the baby so that the birth will be normal. But unless you deliver that baby almost immediately, that child will go back into the breach position because he's comfortable there. He's used to that position.

That's what happened with Peter. Jesus turned him and put him back in position to do God's will, but instead of meditating on Jesus' words to him and adjusting his life and thinking to God's ways and thinking, Peter reverted back to a place of worrying about what Jesus had in mind for John. Would John also feed the sheep? Would John die the way Peter was going to die? What was John supposed to be doing, anyway?

If we do not replace the worried thoughts with God's Word and then continue to move forward in confidence, doing what we are supposed to be doing in the kingdom, then we will look to others and worry about what they are supposed to be doing. We must stick to God's Word and do what He's assigned us to do.

When I'm not fulfilling my assignment, I think about how other people should be doing something to make it better for me. But I am responsible for my life and others are responsible for their lives. I cannot accuse others of not being what they're supposed to be or doing what they're supposed to do because I must focus on who I'm supposed to be and what I'm supposed to do. I have to deal with me. If I deal with me, it will keep me from worrying about you!

Do you really have the mental capacity to handle the mental and emotional strain of your own life AND other people's? I don't have the mental or emotional capacity to do it. I can't handle what Linda's responsible for. I can hardly handle what I've got going on in my life! Therefore, I'm not really interested in being able to look over other people's shoulders and find out if they're doing what God's called them to do. It's all I can do to make sure I'm doing my part.

Unfortunately, when Jesus straightened Peter out, instead of meditating on Jesus' words and renewing his mind, Peter went back to his old competitive habit and focused on John. He used his favor with Jesus to try to learn about something that was none of his business. Jesus knew exactly what was happening and jerked Peter right back into proper position by saying, "If I say that this man is not going to die until I return, what's that to you? You follow Me!" (John 21:22 NLT). In other words, "Peter, don't talk about him. Don't deal with him over issues. Deal with yourself over issues. Your problem is you. Not him."

The greatest problems I've ever faced have not come from any other person on the face of the earth. The greatest problems I have ever faced have been a result of the way I've looked at things when I was not fulfilling my assignment. I accused others of not being to me what they should be, of not doing what they should be doing, when I should have been doing my assignment. I would have had no worry or anxiety if I had judged myself instead of judging others.

> *Judge not, that ye be not judged.*
>
> *For with what judgment ye judge, ye shall be judged: and with what measure ye mete, it shall be measured to you again.*
>
> *And why beholdest thou the mote that is in thy brother's eye, but considerest not the beam that is in thine own eye?*
>
> *Or how wilt thou say to thy brother, Let me pull out the mote out of thine eye; and, behold, a beam is in thine own eye?*
>
> *Thou hypocrite, first cast out the beam out of thine own eye; and then shalt thou see clearly to cast out the mote out of thy brother's eye.*
>
> MATTHEW 7:1-5

I'm not going to judge other people for not being what they're supposed to be because I realize that I am not what I'm supposed to be. Only when I get the two-by-four out of my life will I have enough on the ball to help someone else get the grain of sand out of their eye. God's called me to love people and pray for them and help them by giving them His Word. He hasn't called me to judge them and tell them what to do.

The other side of this third cause of worry, which is to point your finger at someone else because you are not doing your part, is to get your own issues straight with God. Then you can walk in love toward others and really be a blessing to them. If they've messed up, you can go to them in love and say what many good brothers and sisters have said to me through the years. They have looked at me and said, "You know something? You are the greatest guy in the world, but then you do the dumbest thing. Do you realize what you did the other day?"

I answered, "This means you love me, right?"

"Yeah, I love you."

I'm secure because instead of pointing the finger at me in condemnation, they are lovingly helping me to fulfill my assignment, to be who I'm supposed to be. Don't smite me; help me! Don't talk about me; come to me and correct me!

4. Thinking about something we don't have—good or bad.

There is always something we don't have that we can worry about having. When we finally get the thing we were worried about never getting, guess what happens? We find something else to worry about not having. We're like a donkey whose owner sticks a carrot in front of his nose. The donkey keeps walking because he keeps thinking that someday, maybe, he'll catch up to that carrot. The problem is, as long as the donkey is fixed on that carrot, he's not paying attention to where he's going. He doesn't even realize that his owner is leading him to a place he doesn't want to go!

Worrying about what you don't have is a waste of time and effort, and it is a distraction the enemy uses to keep us from all God has for us—where He wants us to go, what He wants us to do, and giving the care and attention to those He connects us to. Jesus said,

> So don't worry about having enough food or drink or clothing.
> Why be like the pagans who are so deeply concerned about these things? Your heavenly Father already knows all your needs,
> and he will give you all you need from day to day if you live for him and make the Kingdom of God your primary concern.
> So don't worry about tomorrow, for tomorrow will bring its own worries. Today's trouble is enough for today.
>
> MATTHEW 6:31-34 NLT

Everything you need will be yours if you don't worry, if you trust God, and if you make the kingdom of God your greatest priority. And remember this: God will meet your need and not your greed. You have to differentiate between need and greed.

God is in the business of meeting your needs as you carry out His will and give Him your whole heart in the process.

We've looked at the positive side of this fourth cause of worry, which is worrying that we won't get the good things in life. The negative side is worrying that we *will* get the terrible things in life. It's still worrying about getting something you will never have, but now we're talking about things like dread diseases and terrorist attacks.

Somebody said to me once, "Doesn't terrorism bother you?"

I said, "No, it doesn't bother me."

"Why doesn't it bother you?"

"Because I pray for my president and all those in authority over me every day. The Bible says we should do this and then we'll live a quiet and peaceful life."

"How can you not worry about it?"

"I think about what I'm responsible for," I answered. "I'm responsible for my home. I'm responsible for my calling. But I'm not responsible for winning the war on terror except when it comes to my duties as a citizen and praying for those who are responsible. When I do what I'm supposed to do and pray for others to be able to do what they're supposed to do, I am in faith, trusting God and His Word. I do not worry."

When it comes to worrying about getting a horrible disease and dying a terrible death, I believe that most people have these kinds of worries. All we have to do is watch medical shows on television or see a movie about someone who dies from a terminal disease, and our minds start racing about something like this happening to us. At times like this we have to go back to God's Word and remember that what He says overrides anything the world says or the television shows us.

He sent his word, and healed them, and delivered them from their destructions.

PSALM 107:20

But he was wounded for our transgressions, he was bruised for our iniquities: the chastisement of our peace was upon him; and with his stripes we are healed.

ISAIAH 53:5

Who his own self bare our sins in his own body on the tree, that we, being dead to sins, should live unto righteousness: by whose stripes ye were healed.

1 PETER 2:24

With the Word of God as our foundation for life, we know that healing is ours, and we don't have to worry about our future. We don't need to worry that we will miss the good things God has for us, and we also don't have to worry that we will be hit with the bad things.

Again, here are the four causes of worry. If you live by God's Word and are led by the Holy Spirit, you can avoid them when worry tries to come into your life.

- Taking authority and responsibility for something that God has not given us authority or responsibility over.
- Relinquishing the authority or responsibility God has given us.
- Not doing the assignment God has given us and pointing to others who aren't doing their assignment.
- Thinking about something we don't have—good or bad.

3

How Did Jesus Deal With Worry?

When you read through the Gospels, you can't help but notice how Jesus continually taught and preached, always trying to pull His disciples into a real life of faith and trust in God and in His Word. In Luke, chapter 10, we are told the story of Mary and Martha. Jesus and a bunch of His followers were visiting them and their brother, Lazarus, in Bethany.

MARY AND MARTHA

Mary didn't want to do anything but sit around and listen to Jesus, the living Word. So Martha complained to Jesus.

> *As Jesus and the disciples continued on their way to Jerusalem, they came to a village where a woman named Martha welcomed them into her home. Her sister, Mary, sat at the Lord's feet, listening to what He taught. But, Martha was worrying over the big dinner she was preparing. She came to Jesus and said, "Lord, doesn't it seem unfair to You that my sister just sits here while I do all the work? Tell her to come and help me.*
>
> LUKE 10:38-40 NLT

Notice Martha said, "Lord, doesn't it seem unfair to You that my sister just sits here while I do all the work?" You can be worried about something and avoid dealing with it by attacking someone else. This happened to me recently when my wife, Linda, was talking to me about a certain situation I was handling in the church. She started to irritate me, and I wanted to just tell her to be quiet and leave me alone.

She stopped talking and asked, "Are you okay?"

Just then I realized that it wasn't Linda who was irritating me. I answered, "Yes, darling. It's nothing."

I was irritated because deep down inside I knew that the way I was handling the situation she was talking about had been worrying me. There was something that was so incorrect and wrong inside me, and the situation was bringing that out. It was my heart that was wrong, not Linda or what she was saying. However, my initial reaction was to get mad at Linda.

That was what was going on with Martha when she complained to Jesus about Mary. Instead of dealing with her worry that everything was not going to get done, she became irritated with Mary for not helping her. But Jesus didn't deal with Martha about Mary; He pointed at the real problem. He said, "My dear Martha, you're so upset over all these details" (Luke 10:41 NLT). He said, "You're worrying about what's not there and what might not happen. You keep worrying about whether or not it's going to be good enough."

Jesus did not tell Martha that attention to detail was wrong. He simply pointed out that she was a worrywart. That was the real issue. Mary should have helped Martha so that both of them would have the opportunity to sit at Jesus' feet and hear the Word. But Jesus was dealing with Martha's problem of worry by saying, "Now look, Martha, you're upset, not only about this but about a lot of things you worry about. You worry too much."

Then Jesus turned His attention to Mary.

> *There is only one thing worth being concerned about. Mary has discovered it. And I won't take it away from her. She discovered the important thing.*

> LUKE 10:43 NLT

Martha needed to learn how to stop worrying, and Jesus gave her the answer: Just be concerned about learning and believing God's Word. Then you won't be worried about everything. Learning and abiding in the Word is the most important thing. It was what Mary had discovered and Jesus would not take that away from her.

First you learn the Word and lay the foundation of your life in the Word. You apply the Word of God to every issue and area of your life. But what many believers do is what Martha did. They take their worry to the Word instead of taking the Word to defeat their worry. They are completely turned around. They say, "Look, I'm right about this and here's why," when they should have filtered the way they felt and thought through the Word of God before they ever said anything to anyone else.

If Martha had examined her thoughts and feelings by the Word of God, she never would have complained to Jesus. She would simply have asked Mary to help her so that everyone could be blessed by both spiritual food and natural food. Then, if Mary had complained to Jesus, He probably would have given her a lesson on being a cheerful servant!

The account of Mary and Martha illustrates that we need to sit at the feet of Jesus and learn of Him, but then faith without works is dead (see James 2:20,26). We must be doers of God's Word and not hearers only. The more we know and study His Word, the more we can be effective in serving Him—and the less we will worry.

I've seen believers either serve God with little knowledge of the Word or sit all the time learning and hearing the Word and never do anything for God or man. In either case, they will end up worrying about their future because they are either working for God without the foundation of His Word or not living according to His Word by acting on it.

As a pastor, I must always make certain that the Word is what I'm giving the people. When I counsel someone, if I just make them feel good I'm not doing them any favors. But if I give them God's Word on their situation, I not only dispel their worries, but I also send them out with a firm foundation to stand on and continue to defeat any worry that would try to come back. Having great people skills is a wonderful gift, but if I'm not doing what I'm doing through the written Word of God, I'm accomplishing absolutely nothing.

I have had tremendous teachers of the Word of God through the years, but it doesn't matter how famous they are or what they said. I cannot base my life on what they said to overcome worry because only God's Word can overcome worry. At the first worrisome thought, I have to be able to say, "It is written…" not what Brother or Sister So-and-so said. This kind of reaction can only happen as I study God's Word like Mary and then act on it like Martha.

When I began to struggle with becoming worry-free forever, I realized I had to get rid of negative thinking. The Bible tells us that we do that by replacing all that negativity with positive, biblical thinking. We drive out the negative thoughts with positive thoughts that are based on God's truth. The negative, evil thinking that has been binding us and hurting us becomes ineffective and disappears as we introduce good, godly thinking into our lives. This is a biblical principle called overcoming evil with good.

> *Be not overcome of evil, but overcome evil with good.*
> ROMANS 12:21

The apostle Paul wasn't telling us just to do more good things than bad things, and then our lives would be okay. What he was saying was that we will not be destroyed by the negative things we've thought and done if we overcome them by thinking and doing good things now and in the future. We overcome evil with good by living in faith, trusting God and His Word. Faith in God dispels fear, and worry is a form of fear.

The Bible says in Hebrews 11:6 that it is impossible to please God without faith. If we are worrying about every little thing that happens or that might happen, we are not living in faith and we are not pleasing God. And the truth is, if we are not pleasing God, there is a good chance we are living miserable lives! I don't know about you, but when I know I'm pleasing God, it doesn't make any difference what my circumstances are because I'm at peace and I have His joy.

This is what Jesus was telling Martha. "Martha, Martha. You need to learn the Word and be filled with faith. Then you won't worry about getting everything done, or what Mary's doing, or whether or not you are pleasing Me. You'll be full of My Word, trusting Me and full of faith, and that is what pleases Me."

If Jesus were standing in front of you right now, and you were literally choking with worry, He would say that knowing and trusting Him and His Word is the only way to stop it. When you do that, the icy fingers of worry will melt away to nothing and you will be able to serve God with joy.

THE DISCIPLES

Jesus made a point of teaching this to His disciples, often putting them through great trials to illustrate that His Word could be trusted, and that He could be trusted.

> And the same day, when the even was come, he saith unto them,
> Let us pass over unto the other side.
> And when they had sent away the multitude, they took him even
> as he was in the ship. And there were also with him other little ships.

21

And there arose a great storm of wind, and the waves beat into the ship, so that it was now full.

And he was in the hinder part of the ship, asleep on a pillow: and they awake him, and say unto him, Master, carest thou not that we perish?

And he arose, and rebuked the wind, and said unto the sea, Peace, be still. And the wind ceased, and there was a great calm.

And he said unto them, Why are ye so fearful? how is it that ye have no faith?

And they feared exceedingly, and said one to another, What manner of man is this, that even the wind and the sea obey him?

MARK 4:35-41

Just after Jesus taught the disciples the greatest parable of all, which is the parable of the sower, He immediately tests them in what they have learned. He had sown the Word into their hearts, and now He was going to show them what kind of ground their hearts were. As it turned out, their hearts had not received very well. Not only were they afraid during the storm, but also they were afraid after the storm because Jesus had delivered them by demonstrating His power over even the wind.

As soon as you learn something new from God's Word, you will be tested on it because the devil comes to steal the Word in your heart. You may be moving forward, have made some good adjustments in your life, and are walking in more peace, when suddenly a great wind whips up and tries to blow that Word right out of your heart, replacing God's peace with demonic fear.

When the storm proved to be a really bad one, the disciples woke up Jesus and accused Him of not caring that they were all going to drown. How did they know that they were going to drown? Because something was speaking to them louder than what they knew about Jesus. And so He asked them, "Why are you so afraid? Do you still not have any faith in Me?"

This reminds us of a verse we talk about a lot in this book. Luke 21:26 says that in the last days when the heavens and earth will be shaken, men's hearts will fail them because of fear. What does the word "fear" really mean? Here is what the dictionary has to say.

> 1 a feeling of anxiety and agitation cause by the presence or nearness of danger, evil, pain, etc.; timidity; dread; terror; fright; apprehension 2 respectful dread; awe; reverence 3 a feeling of uneasiness or apprehension; concern...4 to expect with misgiving; suspect...to be uneasy, anxious, or doubtful.[1]

Fear is the anxiety caused by an expected evil. It's the anxiety that comes when you expect something wrong to happen which hasn't really happened. The word "fear" can also mean timid. It's a painful feeling of impending danger, a fearful expectation.

Jesus spent a lot of time trying to get the disciples to understand that God's Word is trustworthy and He is faithful. He is still trying to get us to understand that today! We are no different from the disciples then. We must believe His Word and have faith in Him to perform His Word to give up worry forever.

The Ultimate Test

I wrote earlier that when we come into a revelation of God's Word, the devil will always come to tempt us to disobey and disbelieve it. This might seem unfair except for one important fact: Jesus already went through everything we will go through.

> *For we have not an high priest which cannot be touched with the feeling of our infirmities; but was in all points tempted like as we are, yet without sin.*
>
> HEBREWS 4:15

Does Jesus understand what you're worrying about? Maybe you think He never dealt with worry. Let me refresh your memory.

> *And he came out, and went, as he was wont, to the mount of Olives; and his disciples also followed him.*
>
> *And when he was at the place, he said unto them, Pray that ye enter not into temptation.*
>
> *And he was withdrawn from them about a stone's cast, and kneeled down, and prayed,*
>
> *Saying, Father, if thou be willing, remove this cup from me: nevertheless not my will, but thine, be done.*
>
> *And there appeared an angel unto him from heaven, strengthening him.*
>
> *And being in an agony he prayed more earnestly: and his sweat was as it were great drops of blood falling down to the ground.*
>
> LUKE 22:39-44

Because Jesus was the Son of God, we think of Him as being a superman without emotions. But Hebrews 4:15 says that He was "touched with the feeling of our infirmities." And when He prayed for God to "remove this cup," there was a reason. He was not being paranoid about being crucified; He had been looking at the certainty of it from before He was even born in human flesh. Now it was right in front of Him.

However you want to categorize what Jesus went through emotionally when He prayed on the Mount of Olives that night, it was so hard that He sweat drops of blood. That means He was experiencing the worst stress a human being can experience. There is no doubt that He went through many emotions, and worry was probably one of them! I mean, if you were facing crucifixion, wouldn't you be worried?

What made Jesus different from the rest of the human race was that even though He experienced all the things and all the emotions that we experience, He didn't sin. In the end He didn't hesitate to say to the Father, "Not my will, but thine, be done." The Bible doesn't say this, but I believe that the moment Jesus said that, the moment He totally committed Himself to the will and Word of God regarding the cross, all worry left Him. He had peace.

> *Looking unto Jesus the author and finisher of our faith; who for the joy that was set before him endured the cross, despising the shame, and is set down at the right hand of the throne of God.*
>
> HEBREWS 12:2

Jesus passed the ultimate test, and He didn't go to the cross being worried about anything. The moment He fully accepted God's will for His life, He had peace about it. It was "for the joy set before him" that He endured the cross. And that's the joy He wants us to walk in every day.

There are lots of things to worry about today. I could take pages of this book and list all the things people have to worry about. But believers are not called to live a life of worry. We're called to live a life of joy and peace by walking in God's will. There's something safe and secure when you know that you're in God's will. No matter how bad things get or how awful you might feel, you are okay inside because you know you're right where you're supposed to be. And if you're right where God wants you to be, then you have the confidence and faith to believe that He's going to get you through to the victory.

If Jesus were standing in the flesh with you right this moment, He would understand what you're worrying about; but He would also help you get rid of it. He would smile and assure you that as a child of God you really have nothing to worry about. All you have to do is walk with Him, talk with Him, let Him speak into your life and change you, have faith in Him, trust and obey His Word, and stay in His will. Then, no matter what you face, you have no worries.

4

Worry Can Bring Tragedy

Sometimes, whether I realize it or not, I worry about the craziest, silliest things because I think about things that I should never think about. For example, it's amazing that if I have a problem with my toe, my mind is able to convince me that I have cancer. Or if I get a flat tire on my car, I think, *What did I do wrong that I got a flat tire?* All of a sudden I think I had better fast for a week to find out how I got out of the will of God. In actual fact, I simply ran over a nail that punctured the tire. Stuff happens, you know. But I'm so worried that my mind immediately decides I'm in sin or out of God's will.

We all do this, don't we? It's part of being human. And Jesus talked about this very thing happening especially in the last days. Let's read two translations of the same verse in the gospel of Luke.

> *The courage of many people will falter because of the fearful fate they see coming upon the earth because the stability of the very heavens will be broken up.*
>
> LUKE 21:26 NLT

> *Men's hearts will fail them for fear of things that are coming upon the earth.*
>
> LUKE 21:26

It is easy to see that what Jesus predicted long ago has come to pass. People all over the world—even believers—are worried about something or someone in their lives.

WORRY AND BAD DECISIONS

I did a little informal study on four different groups of people: 1) high school and college kids, 2) young marrieds, 3) mature adults, and 4) the elderly. I asked them what the number one thing was that they were worried about. I thought it would be interesting to know if their fears and anxieties were different depending on their ages.

The kids in high school and college were primarily uptight about sex and money. They were greatly concerned about getting HIV and AIDS. They wanted to know how they could have sex with anyone they wanted and never get in trouble. They also wanted to know if they and their parents would have enough money for them to go to college.

Young married couples were concerned about their careers in terms of making enough money. They were going after the money rather than simply pursuing their career. They wanted more money and often compromised their belief systems in order to get it.

The mature adults, who are generally those people who have already broken into the field they wanted to break into and are middle-aged, were more concerned about leisure. Did they have enough vacation time? They weren't working to establish their careers; they were working to have the time and money to go on vacation. Their other concern was funding their retirement, which represented permanent leisure activity.

The elderly couples who were of retirement age and beyond had a couple of concerns that relate to each other. The first was whether or not they were going to be able to get prescription drugs, and the second was whether or not Medicare would continue. Both of these worries are about health.

If we look at the worries of each of these four groups, we can see that every one of those worries is a result of poor decisions. Poor decisions create the things that we worry about. Over 90 percent of people who retire in America today retire below the poverty level. That means nine out of ten people who retire, retire with less than $14,000 per year. Consequently, the rest of the citizens of America have to give more to take care of those who made no provision for their retirement. Some seniors were unable to set aside anything through the years because it took their entire income to live. But many simply lived for the moment throughout their lives, not making provision for the future.

A number of years ago there was a family in our congregation who were good people, and a young man in this family died in a car crash. One of the first things the mother did was question why this happened. Why didn't God protect their son? The truth was, the friends this young man was with were drinking. He was a Christian and his mother could not believe her son was drinking. She reasoned that because his friends were not Christians and were drinking, he was just in the wrong place at the wrong time. Sometimes tragedy can be the result of bad judgment or poor choices.

Job had a similar problem with his children because he didn't train or discipline his children to live for God, and all he did was worry about them. When they died, he knew that what he had feared all those years had finally happened. But it wasn't God's fault.

This kind of truth is hard to speak and hard to hear, especially when you have lost a loved one. But when we don't obey God's Word, when we don't do what we know we're supposed to do and what we know is right, it creates an area of worry and fear in our lives that ties God's hands. We are not walking in faith, and when we are not walking in faith, God has nothing to work with. Then the enemy can come in and take advantage of us. He can do great damage to us in that area of worry. This is not God's doing; it is our doing.

Consider what happened to the children of Israel because their faith was overcome by worry. Moses sent twelve spies into the Promised Land to check things out. When they returned, ten of the spies gave what the Bible calls an evil report. All these guys could talk about was how big the giants were and how strong the enemy was. The other two spies, Joshua and Caleb, stuck to God's Word.

> *And Joshua the son of Nun, and Caleb the son of Jephunneh, which were of them that searched the land, rent their clothes:*
>
> *And they spake unto all the company of the children of Israel, saying, The land, which we passed through to search it, is an exceeding good land.*
>
> *If the LORD delight in us, then he will bring us into this land, and give it us; a land which floweth with milk and honey.*
>
> *Only rebel not ye against the LORD, neither fear ye the people of the land; for they are bread for us: their defence is departed from them, and the LORD is with us: fear them not.*
>
> NUMBERS 14:6-9

Fear and worry, doubt and unbelief, are the reasons that most of the children of Israel did not go into the Promised Land. They did not believe the good report of Joshua and Caleb and were afraid of the giants in the land. They let worry and fear choke out the promise of God, and they chose not to trust Him and obey His Word. Worry caused them to make decisions that brought tragedy to their lives. They missed the Promised Land!

And to whom did He swear that they would not enter His rest,
but to those who did not obey?
So we see that they could not enter in because of unbelief.

HEBREWS 3:18,19

Worry, doubt, and unbelief keep us from entering into God's rest and obtaining His blessings for us. On the other hand, when we know we've planted the right things in our lives, that we've meditated God's Word and believed that His Word is going to come to pass, and we've obeyed and lived according to His Word, then we don't have anything to worry about. We can be at peace and rest in the Lord because we have been obedient. We know that everything is going to be all right.

If ye be willing and obedient, ye shall eat the good of the land.

ISAIAH 1:19

The Bible tells us that we can avoid tragedy and live in peace and prosperity if we are willing and obedient to do the commands of God, to follow the leading and guidance of the Holy Spirit instead of our own thinking and desires. We find this in both the Old and New Testaments.

For he that soweth to his flesh shall of the flesh reap corruption;
but he that soweth to the Spirit shall of the Spirit reap life everlasting.

GALATIANS 6:8

When we fill our minds and hearts with God's Word, when we train our children and live our lives according to the Word and the Spirit, we have no reason to worry. We have made the right choices, the wise decisions that avoid tragedy. Worry brings torment, but faith in God to obey His Word brings joy unspeakable and full of glory.

WORRY CAN BE HAZARDOUS TO YOUR HEALTH

There was a time in the Church when, if trouble came to a believer's life, that believer would go to the Word of God and ask the Holy Spirit to show him how to deal with that trouble. Then he would take the Word of God and destroy the attack of the enemy. But over the last fifteen years, I've noticed a difference in how believers handle trouble. More and more Christians are offended and get mad at God when something bad happens to them. "I confessed the Word and put angels around my kids. What happened? Did the angels fall asleep? Why did God let me down?"

We must realize that we live in an adversarial environment where Satan and his demons are hurling bullets, rockets, and every problem under the sun at us. They will take advantage of every weakness—and worry is a weakness. Worry can harass you so much and so hard that it causes you to do things you never would ordinarily think of doing. Worry can cause your mind to spin out of control. You think weird things and then do the unthinkable.

One of the most obvious and common areas where I see this happening is in the area of healing. When believers are young and healthy, healing comes easy because the body is stronger and younger. But when they get in their mid-thirties or forties and the vehicle they've been running in requires a lot more maintenance and attention, they begin to question God's Word on healing.

As you age, broken bones don't heal as quickly, muscles are very sore after working in the yard, and it's a major battle to maintain that perfect shape you took pride in all through the years. In fact, the "battle of the bulge" is one you seem to lose more than win!

Gone are the days of just bouncing back from an injury or a few weeks of eating junk food. When the alarm clock goes off in the morning, instead of jumping out of bed, we carefully sit up first. Then we get up real slowly to minimize the stiffness and keep us from getting dizzy. And if we stop to think about how our bodies are getting looser, weaker, and wrinkled (all over!), we become worried about our future. If we feel like this in middle age, how will we feel in old age? How can we get to old age? Do we even want old age?

The problem with worry is that it can cause physical changes in your body that you don't realize. I found a great Web site on the Internet one day. It's called the Worry Website (I'm not joking—look it up). It says that every system in our bodies is affected by worry. In addition to raising blood pressure and increasing blood clotting, worry can prompt the liver to produce more cholesterol, all of which can raise the risk of heart attack and stroke.

Worry can impact your respiratory system and aggravate asthma. Growing evidence even suggests that chronic worry can compromise your immune system, making you more vulnerable to bacteria and viruses and perhaps even cancer. Muscle tension caused by worry can give rise to headaches, back pain, and other body aches.

Worry can also trigger an increase in stomach acid and either slow down or speed up muscle constrictions in your intestines. Consequently, worry can cause you to have stomachaches, diarrhea, heartburn, and gas, and can even affect your skin. I couldn't believe the rash I saw on a lady one day. I said to her, "How in the world did that happen?"

She said, "It just happened yesterday. I'm under a lot of stress."

Her rash caused me to question how worry can affect the different parts of the body. Worry causes physical stress, and stress causes the body to do funny things to get rid of it. When I get stressed my neck gets tight. I feel like somebody needs to hit it with a hammer. Most of us aren't aware that we are stressed until it shows up in a physical symptom like an ache or pain.

After years of dealing with worry and trying to help others deal with it, it suddenly occurred to me one day that worry was dangerous. What I was thinking was nothing new to God, of course.

> A merry heart doeth good like a medicine: but a broken spirit drieth the bones.
>
> PROVERBS 17:22

A merry heart is not a worrying heart. A merry heart is full of faith in God's Word and the power of the Holy Spirit to lead us, guide us, and keep us healthy. As we get older, the challenge to remain healthy and productive becomes greater, but our faith and wisdom from God's Word and our ability to walk in the Spirit also grow stronger. Paul wrote about this in his second letter to the Corinthians.

> But though our outward man perish, yet the inward man is renewed day by day.
>
> For our light affliction, which is but for a moment, worketh for us a far more exceeding and eternal weight of glory;
>
> While we look not at the things which are seen, but at the things which are not seen: for the things which are seen are temporal; but the things which are not seen are eternal.
>
> 2 CORINTHIANS 4:16-18

Notice how Paul dealt with his outward man perishing. He focused on eternal things. He reminded himself that his inward man was stronger than ever in God's Word and in the power of the Holy Spirit. If he were alive today, Paul would probably be very diligent to exercise, eat correctly, and abstain from habits like smoking or taking drugs that would hurt his physical body. But he would also be quick to say that a believer could do all these good things to keep physically healthy and still become sick with worry.

We must be good stewards of the bodies God has given us, but the best thing we can do to keep ourselves healthy is to defeat every worry that tries to capture our imagination and destroy our lives. We must recognize the enemy's lies and kick them out of our minds forever.

> *For though we walk in the flesh, we do not war after the flesh:*
>
> *(For the weapons of our warfare are not carnal, but mighty through God to the pulling down of strong holds;)*
>
> *Casting down imaginations, and every high thing that exalteth itself against the knowledge of God, and bringing into captivity every thought to the obedience of Christ.*
>
> 2 CORINTHIANS 10:3-5

Ask the Holy Spirit to pinpoint any thought that involves worry, and then cast it down. Replace that lie of the enemy with the life-giving, redeeming Word of God. And when aging tries to frighten you or cause you to worry about the future, turn your attention to the eternal things, the eternal weight of glory that awaits you.

Nowhere in the Word of God do we find that God's Word is only true for believers of a certain age. "By His stripes you were healed" is true whether you are twenty years old or ninety years old. You may have more challenges in your physical body at ninety, and you might have to make adjustments for aging, but you don't have to be sick and diseased.

For the kingdom of God is not meat and drink; but righteousness, and peace, and joy in the Holy Ghost.

ROMANS 14:17

This verse of Scripture tells us two important things. First, the kingdom is not in meat and drink. Meat and drink affect our physical well being, and we should be wise about this, but the kingdom of God always governs the physical kingdom of our flesh.

Second, the kingdom of God is not a place of worry but of righteousness, peace, and joy in the Holy Spirit. As long as we are walking in the Spirit and not according to the flesh, as long as we believe the report of the Lord (His Word) over any other report, we will not worry. We must continuously guard our hearts and minds so that righteousness, peace, and joy in the Holy Ghost reign over whatever is taking place in our physical bodies.

Worry cannot invade our lives to cause tragedy if we make godly decisions according to the Word and the Spirit of God. Nor can worry mess up our body chemistry and cause all kinds of symptoms if we keep our minds and hearts on the Word and the Spirit. When God is truly our final authority, we will live free of worry.

5

Five Things That Drive Out Worry

How do we fix the problem of chronic worrying? This is something I asked myself when I was first born again. Following are five things that I found to stop worry from grabbing me by the throat.

1. THINK LIKE GOD

Do you want to know what I think? No. I don't even want to know what I think. Why? Because I'm ignorant and carnal. What has caused me more pain than anything else in my entire life is I. I have hurt myself more than any person I know. I have made wrong decisions. I've gone to places I shouldn't have. I've hung around people I shouldn't have. I've done things that I shouldn't have done. And the consequences were not pleasant.

There are consequences for our actions. If we do not renew our minds with God's Word so that we embrace God's thoughts and act like Him, then those actions are not going to bring good consequences. God's grace and mercy can alleviate them when we repent and serve Him with our whole heart, but most of the time we do the crime and then we do the time.

David and Bathsheba's baby was conceived in adultery and died. Samson messed around with Delilah and told her his secret, and he did not grow new eyes after the Philistines gouged them out. His strength only returned long enough for him to kill more Philistines and then die. There are always consequences to everything we do. And everything we do began with a thought.

Our actions are the result of what we think. That's why the Bible stresses the point that we must renew our minds continually with God's Word so we can think like God. When we think like God, then we will act like God. Thinking like God is not worrying!

> *So, here's what I want you to do, God helping you. Taking your every day, ordinary life, your sleeping, eating, going to work and walking around life, and place it before God as an offering. Embracing what God does for you is the best thing you can do for Him.*
>
> *Don't become so well adjusted to your culture that you fit into it without even thinking. Instead, fix your attention on God, you'll be changed from the inside out, readily recognize what He wants from you and quickly respond to it - unlike the culture around you - always dragging you down to it's level of immaturity, God brings the best out of you and He develops well-formed maturity in you.*
>
> ROMANS 12:1,2 MESSAGE

The New Living Translation of verse 2 says, "Don't copy the behavior and the customs of this world. But let God transform you into a new person by changing the way that you think. Then, you will know what God wants you to do." Our culture wants us to watch television hours a day, become obsessed with sports, eat junk food, hang out with ungodly friends, drink beer, and smoke. But God's culture involves reading and studying His Word, praying privately and corporately, fellowshipping with other believers, and reaching out to the lost.

If you are avoiding God's culture and taking part in the world's culture, you are probably walking in deception and doing things that are not godly or God's will for your life. How do I know this? Because if you don't begin to think like God, you're not going to act like God. And you don't think like God without being transformed by His Word on a daily basis.

This is step number one in driving out worry because nothing happens to you in the kingdom of God if you don't get transformed by God's Word and think like Him. You will continue to worry and try to fix things in your own thinking and ability—and mess everything up—as long as you avoid being transformed by the Word of God. (And by the way, God doesn't take you to step number five until the first four steps are completed.)

The Bible says, "Don't copy the behavior and customs of this world, but let God transform you into a new person by changing the way that you think. Then, you will know what God wants you to do and how good and how pleasing and how perfect His will really is." You'll know what God wants you to do because you will be thinking like He thinks. And when you think His thoughts, you won't be worrying.

2. THINK ON GOOD THINGS

Most of us spend more time thinking about all the problems in our lives than all the good things God is doing in our lives. But the Bible tells us to do just the opposite. I found that when I started thinking more about the good things God is doing than the bad things I was facing, I worried a lot less about my life and everyone involved in it.

> *Finally, brethren, whatsoever things are true, whatsoever things are honest, whatsoever things are just, whatsoever things are pure, whatsoever things are lovely, whatsoever things are of good report; if there be any virtue, and if there be any praise, think on these things.*
> PHILIPPIANS 4:8

The key here is the phrase "good report." Think about the good report and then no bad report can worry you. Right now I'm thinking in terms of gossip. God hates gossip because it divides His people and causes terrible damage to them in the process. Gossip kills, steals, and destroys because it agrees with the accuser of the brethren, who kills, steals, and destroys. When you worry and then gossip about someone, you are agreeing with Satan as he accuses your brother or sister. You are causing division in the body of Christ when you gossip.

It is so important to stick with the good report from God! But you cannot do that if you don't think on what is true, honest, just, pure, lovely, virtuous, and all that is praiseworthy. If the Holy Spirit gives you a heads up that a brother or sister is overtaken in a fault, don't worry or gossip about it! Handle it scripturally.

> *Don't worry about anything; instead, pray about everything. Tell God what you need, and thank him for all he has done.*
>
> *If you do this, you will experience God's peace, which is far more wonderful than the human mind can understand. His peace will guard your hearts and minds as you live in Christ Jesus.*
>
> PHILIPPIANS 4:6-8 NLT

Don't worry—pray! Pray for the one you are tempted to worry and gossip about. And if the Holy Spirit leads you to go to them, go with a humble and teachable spirit because otherwise you will fall into judgementalism and say and do something worse than they said or did. (See Galatians 6:1.) If you find yourself worrying about someone, hit your knees and pray! Get God's good report. Not only will you have nothing to worry about, but also you will defeat gossip and division and bring healing and restoration to a brother or sister in the Lord.

3. SEE THE ETERNAL REALITY

Reality lives just beyond your natural ability to see. Reality is found in God's Word as the Holy Spirit reveals it to you spiritually. To drive worry out of your life, you can't dwell on the circumstances you are in but let the Holy Spirit show you the eternal things that are the reality of your life.

> *For our present troubles are quite small and won't last very long. Yet they produce for us an immeasurably great glory that will last forever!*
>
> *So we don't look at the troubles we can see right now; rather, we look forward to what we have not yet seen. For the troubles we see will soon be over, but the joys to come will last forever.*
>
> 2 CORINTHIANS 4:17,18 NLT

The *King James Version* says it this way: "While we look not at the things that are seen, but we look at the things that are not seen." Focusing on your circumstances is not wise because they change continually. Just when you think you have one problem figured out, another comes along. Therefore, all you do is worry. When you look at the problem it produces worry. But when you look at what the Word of God says about the problem, it produces peace. The Word of God reigns over your circumstances because His Word is eternal and your circumstances are temporary. The Word enables you to look beyond them into the eternal truths that will never change. Those truths dispel all worry.

Reality lives just beyond your natural sight, so look into spiritual truth through the eyes of faith. Second Corinthians 5:7 says that we walk by faith and not by sight. *The New Living Translation* says, "That is why we live by believing and not by seeing." Don't look at the things that you face; look at the things that are eternal. When you see the eternal reality, you will drive worry out of your life.

4. THROW YOUR WORRIES ON GOD

God is big enough to carry whatever is worrying you! In 1 Peter, chapter 5, Peter talks about worry in terms of fulfilling our calling and purpose. He talks about serving our leaders faithfully and trusting God to promote us. He talks about being humble before God and literally throwing all of our cares about our future onto God's back.

> *You younger men, accept the authority of the elders. And all of you, serve each other in humility, for "God sets himself against the proud, but he shows favor to the humble."*
>
> *So humble yourselves under the mighty power of God, and in his good time he will honor you.*
>
> *Give all your worries and cares to God, for he cares about what happens to you.*
>
> 1 PETER 5:5-7 NLT

Submitting to the leadership in your life produces a good attitude in your heart. You are humble and develop faith and trust in God to guide your leaders and take care of you. Whenever you break away from the leadership God has placed you under, it produces a bad attitude. You do not trust, and instead you worry. It's impossible to throw your worries on the Lord when you are arrogant and rebellious.

When you trust God to lead your leaders and protect you from their mistakes, when you humble yourself and stay teachable, then you are walking in faith and you have the favor of God on you. The Bible says that He takes delight in the humble but turns away from the proud. So you have His favor when you stay humble before Him. With that attitude of heart, whatever happens, you can easily drive out worry.

And you who are younger must follow your leaders. But all of you, leaders and followers alike, are to be down to earth with each other, for—

"God has had it with the proud,

But takes delight in just plain people."

So be content with who you are, and don't put on airs. God's strong hand is on you; he'll promote you at the right time. Live carefree before God; he is most careful with you.

1 PETER 5:5-7 MESSAGE

God takes delight in regular people who tell the truth. When the time is right, He'll bring you out of this situation, He'll promote you, He'll vindicate you, and He'll give you the victory. This scripture pictures God as a loving father that carries every care and worry and fear we throw at Him. He said, "Give it to Me! I'll carry it for you. And then I'll exalt you when the time is right." When you relax and keep your eyes on God, you won't be worrying.

5. KEEP MOVING AHEAD IN GOD'S WILL

You can tell when someone is overcome with worry and fear because they stop doing what God has called them to do. They just shut down. They may talk a good game, but nothing happens. I tell my congregation to look at a person's feet instead of listening to their mouth to find out where that person really is. If they are in faith, they will be walking forward in God's will for their lives. If they are worried and scared, they will be standing still and going nowhere fast.

Girls, do you want to find out if a man is real? Watch his feet. Don't listen to him. He could be lying. I know because I used to lie all the time. I told my schoolteacher that my grandmother died five times. She finally asked me, "How many grandmas you got?" When I was late for a date with Linda, I told her I had to bail a friend out of jail. After we got married, I tried to tell her the truth, but by then she had a hard time believing me because of all the lies I had already told her. Jesus made the difference. When I began to follow Jesus and obey His Word, she began to believe me and trust me.

> *But be ye doers of the word, and not hearers only, deceiving your own selves.*

> JAMES 1:22

The person who is the most deceived by their own words is the person who talks a big game but does nothing. He'll tell you all the things God has called him to do but nothing ever materializes. Six months later he's still talking but he has nothing to show you. Unless his actions follow his words, he's deceiving himself, and at the root of all of that deception and empty talk is a huge pot of worry.

You will do nothing but worry if you don't act on God's Word. If you are worrying, check and see if there is something God has told you to do that you haven't done or if there is something He wants to clean up in your life. Then reverse your course and become a doer of the Word. I guarantee you that you will stop worrying and you will have no need to tell tall tales and deceive yourself. Moving forward in God's will drives out all worry.

I encourage you to stop right now and pray. Ask God to show you in what areas of your life you are worrying and need to

1 think like God,

2 think on good things,

3 see the eternal reality,

4 throw your worries on God, and

5 keep moving forward in God's will.

6

What Job Teaches About Worry

No book in the Bible causes believers more worry than the book of Job. In the first three chapters of the book of Job, you can see that absolutely horrible things happened to him. When I was a new Christian, I changed the "J" in Job to an "R" and made it the book of Rob because my life seemed to be on the same track as his was. Everything that could go wrong went wrong. Just when I thought things couldn't get any worse, things got worse. Bad things happen to good people, and I was afraid. After all, I was a mess and the Bible says that Job was the most righteous man on the face of the earth.

THE CONTROVERSY

Then the Lord said to Satan, "Have you considered My servant Job, that there is none like him on the earth, a blameless and upright man, one who fears God and shuns evil?"

JOB 1:8 NKJV

Job was a guy who really wanted to do the right thing. His heart was right with God, and God actually boasted about him to Satan. Job was God's poster child for righteousness. But then Satan challenged God on this.

So Satan answered the Lord and said, "Does Job fear God for nothing?

"Have You not made a hedge around him, around his household, and around all that he has on every side? You have blessed the work of his hands, and his possessions have increased in the land.

"But now, stretch out Your hand and touch all that he has, and he will surely curse You to Your face!"

JOB 1:9-11 NKJV

When I first read this I thought God would come up with some wise and incredible answer that would tell Satan to mind his own business. Instead, to my horror and amazement, God said something totally different.

And the Lord said to Satan, "Behold, all that he has is in your power, only do not lay a hand on his person."

JOB 1:12 NKJV

To me and probably to you, this can be one of the most worrisome statements we read in the Bible, depending on how we look at it. One perspective sees that God may remove His hedge of protection whether we are being obedient or not, but He does it to prove our faith and always restores in the end. Another perspective sees that God is in charge and Satan can't do anything to us unless God gives him permission, and that gives a great deal of comfort because we know God loves us.

All this comes down to what the Bible says. God states that Job is righteous and that he fears Him. But then He also says that all Job possesses is in Satan's power. The only protection He provides for Job is for his person. Let's see what happened to Job.

- Job 1:13-15 The Sabeans stole his donkeys and oxen and killed his servants who attended them.

- Job 1:16 The fire of God consumed his sheep and the servants attending them.

- Job 1:17 The Chaldeans stole his camels and killed the servants attending them.

- Job 1:18-19 A great wind collapsed the oldest son's house where all of Job's children were partying and killed them all.

Job reacts in a very pious, faithful way. He says:

> *"Naked I came from my mother's womb,*
> *And naked shall I return there.*
> *The Lord gave, and the Lord has taken away;*
> *Blessed be the name of the Lord."*
>
> JOB 1:21 NKJV

Job refuses to blame God or become bitter toward Him for all his losses and suffering. The Bible goes on to say in verse 22, "In all this Job did not sin nor charge God with wrong." So Job is still a good guy in all respects. But Satan is not satisfied and comes to God again.

> Then the Lord said to Satan, "Have you considered My servant Job, that there is none like him on the earth, a blameless and upright man, one who fears God and shuns evil? And still he holds fast to his integrity, although you incited Me against him, to destroy him without cause."
>
> So Satan answered the Lord and said, "Skin for skin! Yes, all that a man has he will give for his life.
>
> "But stretch out Your hand now, and touch his bone and his flesh, and he will surely curse You to Your face!"
>
> And the Lord said to Satan, "Behold, he is in your hand, but spare his life."
>
> JOB 2:3-6 NKJV

At this point in the story, I hoped that Job would prove God's point to Satan and I wouldn't have to in my lifetime!

> *So Satan went out from the presence of the Lord, and struck Job*
> *with painful boils from the sole of his foot to the crown of his head.*
>
> JOB 2:7 NKJV

Now Job is not only suffering because of the loss of his children, his livestock, and his servants, but he is in intense physical pain as well. His wife tells him to curse God and die, and Job is probably wondering why she wasn't in the house that collapsed and killed his children. But he still maintains that God is God and He can do what He wants.

> *"Shall we indeed accept good from God, and shall we not accept*
> *adversity?" In all this Job did not sin with his lips.*
>
> JOB 2:9 NKJV

According to the Bible and God's testimony to Satan, Job never sinned and is still not sinning. He has done nothing to deserve all this heartache; yet God allowed it. Then Job's friends show up. He's probably thinking that they'll be sympathetic and have some wisdom and encouragement for him, unlike his wife. He's thinking, *Finally, there's a friend that sticks closer than a wife.*

Instead of wise words of comfort, however, Job's friends start telling him where he is wrong. Of course, the only logical explanation is that he's got problems or this wouldn't have happened to him. Now he has lost all his worldly possessions, his children are dead, his wife wishes he were dead, he is in intense physical pain, and his friends are asking him for a laundry list of his sins against God. Is there anything else that can go wrong?

The controversy surrounding Job is timeless and will go on until Jesus comes and straightens us out. Did God allow an innocent, righteous man to suffer just so He could win a bet with Satan, or did Job actually do something that put him and all that concerned him in Satan's power? Did God put Job in Satan's power, or did Job put himself in Satan's power?

JOB FEARED MORE THAN GOD

The Bible is clear that Job was blameless and sinless, so we cannot say that sin allowed Satan to kill, steal, and destroy in Job's life. And God is not vindictive and wicked, enjoying the suffering we go through. So why did all this happen to Job?

> *"For the thing I greatly feared has come upon me,*
> *And what I dreaded has happened to me.*
> *I am not at ease, nor am I quiet;*
> *I have no rest, for trouble comes.*
>
> JOB 3:15,16 NKJV

Job may not have been sinning, but he lived with an undercurrent of worry in his life that turned into fear. He spent his days worrying that everything he enjoyed in life—his family, his servants, his wealth, his friends, his good health—would one day be taken away from him. His faith in God made him righteous, but he still worried that God might require everything from him. He feared God in a righteous way, but he also was afraid for himself and what concerned him.

I believe some things happen in my life because I give permission for them to happen. I create a doorway, either good or bad, through my feelings, attitudes, thoughts, words, or actions. When something bad happens, I ask myself: How did this happen? Have I been rebellious or fearful about some issue? Did I do something in ignorance of God's Word? There are times when I have nothing to do with creating a situation. I just walk into it. But other times I am the cause of what is happening to me.

The devil may bring persecution into my life for righteousness sake, but I have to give it permission to remain there. I have to provide a doorway for that thing to continue operating in my life. I believe Job's doorway is found in chapter 3, where he says that what he had been worrying about for years has come upon him. Job feared losing his family and material goods more than he feared God, and that was Satan's doorway to cause destruction in his life.

WHAT SHOULD WE THINK ABOUT JOB?

If everything Job feared came upon him, then it is easy to know what he dreaded. Losing his livestock, the death of his children and servants, physical pain and disease, his friends thinking he's a sinner, natural disasters like wind and fire, and attacks from people like the Chaldeans and Sabeans. It looks like Job was afraid of everything except losing his wife, and we can understand why!

But there is something more to this, and it is what every believer worries about. Job was afraid that God would take everything from him, that one day God would say, "Job, you are righteous because you believe in Me, but now I want to see just how much you trust Me. So I'm going to allow the devil to come in and steal, kill, and destroy. Then we will see if your faith and trust in Me is based on what I've given you or who I am."

Every Christian who has read the book of Job has worried about this! We read the book and we get uptight that someday the bottom is going to fall out from underneath us because God wants to see if we really love Him more than anything or anyone else in our lives, more than His blessings. To make matters worse, then we start worrying about whether or not we would be able to stand strong in the Lord if we did lose everything.

So how do we handle this worry? What is the answer? Like everything else, we find it in God's Word.

For God is greater than our hearts, and he knows everything.
1 John 3:20 NLT

First of all, God doesn't need to find out if we are completely sold out to Him because He already knows! He already knows what we've surrendered to Him and what we are still holding back. So He's not going to take everything from us to see what we will say and do because He already knows what we will say and do.

Second, when Satan challenged God about Job, Jesus had not yet come. After Jesus died on the cross and was resurrected from the dead, the Bible says that God was totally satisfied that sin had been paid for, that Jesus stripped the devil and all his demons of their authority, and that through Jesus we no longer fear death and destruction because of it.

Forasmuch then as the children are partakers of flesh and blood, he also himself likewise took part of the same; that through death he might destroy him that had the power of death, that is, the devil.
Hebrews 2:14

And having spoiled principalities and powers, he made a show of them openly, triumphing over them in it.
Colossians 2:15

Satan is called the accuser of the brethren, the one who held men, women, and children in the bondage of fearing death all their lives. Before I was saved, I was really afraid of dying. I worried about it constantly. But after I was saved, death was no longer an issue because I knew I was living forever, and when I died I would just change addresses from earth to heaven—and heaven is a whole lot better than earth!

What I'm saying here is that because Jesus paid the debt for our sin and the devil was finally put in his place, God doesn't need to brag about people like Job or you or me. Now, when Satan comes to accuse any of us, God will just point to Jesus! Jesus did it all for all of us. But there's more!

As believers and children of God, we have a better covenant with better promises than Job had in the Old Covenant. We have the Holy Spirit living in us, and we have the Word of God that explains who we are in Christ and our authority over the enemy. But we also understand the bottom line. Paul said it best.

> *While we live, we live to please the Lord. And when we die, we go to be with the Lord. So in life and in death, we belong to the Lord.*
> *Christ died and rose again for this very purpose, so that he might be Lord of those who are alive and of those who have died.*
>
> ROMANS 14:8,9 NLT

Whether we live or die, we are the Lord's. Everything we are and do and have is His. I love my wife and my children, but they aren't mine; they are His. I love my congregation, but they belong to Jesus. I enjoy having a nice home and a great car and nice clothes to wear, but it all belongs to the Lord, and if He says, "Give your house to John and Betty," then I give my house to John and Betty.

Job didn't understand that everything was God's to begin with. He didn't have the assurance that he would see his children and servants again in heaven. He didn't know that through the blood and name of Jesus Christ we have authority over sickness and disease. But most of all, he didn't know that through Jesus God would be totally satisfied and not require sacrifice from human beings anymore. In fact, God never really liked sacrifice. What He has always desired was that we fear

Him, reverence Him, love Him with our whole hearts, and obey His Word and Spirit.

> *For thou desirest not sacrifice; else would I give it: thou delightest not in burnt offering.*
> *The sacrifices of God are a broken spirit: a broken and a contrite heart, O God, thou wilt not despise.*
>
> PSALM 51:16,17

> *And Samuel said, Hath the LORD as great delight in burnt offerings and sacrifices, as in obeying the voice of the LORD? Behold, to obey is better than sacrifice, and to hearken than the fat of rams.*
>
> 1 SAMUEL 15:22

When I saw this in the Word of God, I was set free from worrying that God was going to take everything from me. My life is His. My family is His. My church is His. My ministry is His. My worldly possessions are His. And whatever He wants to do with them is fine with me. Whatever He wants me to do with them, I will do it because my heart is His. I don't have to be worrying about what He's going to require of me because it's all His already.

So don't go around worrying that you are the next Job! You are God's child and He's going to talk to *you* about your life, *not* to Satan. You have a better covenant and better promises. You have authority over the enemy. Your name is written in the Lamb's Book of Life. Everything you are and do and have is God's, which means your life is in the hands of your loving Father.

7

Worry and Obsession

If you do not immediately deal with the first thought of worry and instead begin to meditate on it, it will become your master. I know that this is true for me. I remember the day the thought came to me, *I pray that the devil doesn't find out about this part of my life because if he does, I think he could knock me over with a feather.* I'd been standing so hard and so long over certain issues, punching my way through, and then all of a sudden the day came when I felt like I was too weak. That's when I had the thought that if the devil knew how I felt at that moment, he could take me in a second.

I thank God I didn't accept that worry into my life. I didn't want that to happen and I refused it. That was a real victory for me at the time. It wasn't the kind where you shout; it was the kind of victory where you move from one level of maturity to the next by a simple, quiet resolve not to do anything other than what God's Word says.

> *For though we walk in the flesh, we do not war after the flesh:*
> *(For the weapons of our warfare are not carnal, but mighty through God to the pulling down of strong holds;)*
> *Casting down imaginations, and every high thing that exalteth itself against the knowledge of God, and bringing into captivity every thought to the obedience of Christ.*
> 2 CORINTHIANS 10:3-5

We have to deal with worry and fear by waging war against them. We must be resolved to continue to cast those worrisome thoughts down again and again until they are finally defeated forever. If we don't become filled with God's Word, then we will become obsessed with worry. When I tell believers this, some actually say, "Well, I tried that, but it doesn't work."

My answer to them is, "No, you are quitting in the middle of the battle because it takes time to free our mind of worry and replace those negative thoughts with God's Word. You see, you don't just get rid of the bad thoughts; you must also begin to meditate in God's thoughts."

We fight the same kind of battle to make our lives a living sacrifice of praise unto the Lord. "Well, I don't want to lift my hands to God. I will be a hypocrite if I raise my hands when I don't feel like it." No, you won't be a hypocrite if you raise your hands. You'll be obedient to God's Word by offering yourself as a sacrifice of praise to the Lord. And then your obedience to God's Word will bring forth a willingness, and once you're willing you'll start getting free. Your spirit will begin to overwhelm your carnal, fleshly desires. You will begin to experience the peace and joy of God's presence and enter into worship.

Entering into worship is another way that we can rid ourselves of obsessive worry. It is extremely important that we do this. Remember Job? He continued to worry about his children, his servants, his livestock, his health, and all the blessings God had given him. He allowed himself to be dominated by thoughts of worry, always wondering if one day he would wake up and God would have taken everything from him.

Whatever you worry about will dominate your thinking and may even determine your destination. Even though you don't want something to happen, if you continuously worry about it, you can draw that calamity to yourself. You can create a doorway for the enemy to steal, kill, and destroy. Like Job, what you most feared can come upon you. This is why it is so important to cast down and refuse to give place to any thoughts of worry or fear.

THE GENERATION FACTOR

Some obsessive worry can be generational. Look at your mother and father, your brothers and sisters, your grandparents and great-grandparents, and even your aunts and uncles and cousins. Do you see a pattern of certain fears and worries in your family? So often we just accept these "family traits" as the way it has to be because that's the way our family has always been. In fact, we often get offended if anyone suggests it doesn't have to be that way.

When the Holy Spirit gives someone a word of knowledge that we are struggling because of a family trait of worrying about something, we get angry and defensive. We think they are putting down our family and we take it personally. The truth is, every family has issues God wants to deal with, and He's probably going to send other believers to help us get over these issues. We need to recognize that help and not push them away. Recognizing the problem and pinpointing that issue is half the battle in defeating worry that has held a family in bondage for generations.

The reason why we argue or disagree with people about our issues—and everybody has issues—is because we worship them. That may sound ridiculous, but remember what an "issue" is. An issue is something that was instilled in you from the time you were born because it was established in your family from generations past. That worry is part of your family's identity. "Oh well, hypochondria just runs in our family. That's who we are! We just think we've got one sickness after another."

Worry is just as dangerous a family trait as alcoholism or drug abuse. And that brings us to the point that it is easy to worry about all the negative family traits we inherit. One of the things that I had to come to grips with in my life was that I had a weakness toward alcohol and drug abuse. My mother was a drug addict before it was popular. When I was growing up you could go to as many doctors as you wanted to and get as many prescriptions as you could get the doctors to write. And those doctors could prescribe some really good drugs! My mother could get a year's supply of drugs in a couple of weeks by just going from doctor to doctor with the same complaint.

She began with diuretics, which are basically just speed. When Linda and I were first married, I used to get a hundred to three hundred hits of speed and do them until they were gone. I would be up days at a time while I was working, cutting meat, and I'm telling you that I've got scars to prove it! But one day I recognized that I had a propensity toward drug abuse, so I stopped it altogether. Today I don't take an aspirin unless I absolutely have to because I know that I have a generational weakness in that area. I also will never sniff the cork of a bottle of alcohol or beer. Why? My grandfather on my mother's side died of cirrhosis of the liver at the age of forty-four. My father was an alcoholic and had a number of siblings who were also alcoholics.

Because my mother was a gypsy, I'm very sensitive to any occult issues. My father and mother both had to deal with bouts of mental illness, there were family members who had to be institutionalized because of mental problems, and I was no exception. I recognize that all of these issues are in my family, and I have had and continue to have to deal with any worry concerning them. I also have to recognize that I cannot handle these issues by myself.

Obviously, I had a lot to worry about! It wasn't hard for me to feel like I was being choked and strangled by the possibility of being a drug addict, an alcoholic, a mental patient, and completely carried away and deceived by occult spirits. If I had not decided to fight the worry and fear associated with these generational issues, and if I had not accepted the help that God offered to me through the body of Christ, I would probably not be writing this book about it today.

Accepting God's Help in Human Form

Human beings often act really funny when they get in a serious situation. For example, when a person is drowning, and a lifeguard swims out to rescue them, they will try to beat up the very person who is trying to save them! They are so overtaken with fear that they believe the lifeguard is trying to drown them. So lifeguards are trained to take them underwater and hold them at arms' length until they stop flailing and thrashing around. Then, when they stop swinging their arms, you take hold of them properly, bring them to the surface, and pull them to safety. If you don't do this, both of you could drown.

The same is true with spiritual danger. You might see that worry is choking and strangling someone, but until they come to the end of themselves and realize that they need help, they are going to be working against you if you try to help them. You have to wait until they have exhausted themselves and are willing to work with you. Then you can help them so that the Word and the Spirit can set them free.

> And let us consider one another to provoke unto love and to good works:
> Not forsaking the assembling of ourselves together, as the manner of some is; but exhorting one another: and so much the more, as ye see the day approaching.
> HEBREWS 10:24,25

The Bible tells us to "consider one another." All of us have underlying worries and fears that we may not even recognize. That's why God put us in the body of Christ and connected us as a family. We have to help each other identify these demonic strongholds, tear them down, and build a fortress of God's Word that will keep them out forever. We need one another.

> Bear ye one another's burdens, and so fulfil the law of Christ.
> GALATIANS 6:2

There are times in our lives when we must trust someone enough to be able to tell us the truth. I have to trust Linda enough for her to tell me the truth. Linda has to trust me enough for me to tell her the truth. God has put us together and we fulfill the law Christ, the law of love, by loving each other enough to tell each other the truth. We are honest with one another but in love. We help each other to see the truth and face the truth. Then God's truth sets us free.

> But speaking the truth in love, may grow up into him in all things, which is the head, even Christ.
> EPHESIANS 4:15

It's hard to face the truth sometimes. We don't like to even consider that there might be something wrong in the way we are thinking and acting. And being believers, we don't like to admit that we are worried about anything. We like to see ourselves as great men and women of faith who are never moved by anything but the Word and Spirit of God. But in order to grow up and be great men and women of God, in order to "grow up into him in all things," we have to listen to the ones God has put in our lives.

If I even try to get obsessed with something that is worrying me, Linda is there to speak the truth in love to me. Why? Because I probably don't even see what's going on with me. I may know that I don't have peace and that I'm spinning my wheels trying to get things done but not getting anywhere, but I have no real understanding of what's hindering me. I can't see the forest for the trees.

Linda considers me, prays for me, and asks God for wisdom on how to approach me, because she's the lifeguard who doesn't want to be drowned by the person she's trying to rescue. And this is very important because God is the only one who can rescue someone. If you don't give Him the situation and get His Word and wisdom on how to handle it, you might drown along with the person you are trying to help.

You might be thinking that Linda knows all my weaknesses and really has a lot on me, but I've got the goods on her too! She knows my weaknesses and I know hers. She knows what worries me and I know what worries her. No one is any better than anyone else because we have all sinned and fallen short of the glory of God. We all have issues that worry us. We all have generational issues that worry us.

Linda is a unique mixture because one of her parents is Polish and the other is Italian. Do you know what that does to you? It confuses you! She'll say, "We're having people over and I've got to cook dinner."

"How many people you gonna cook dinner for?" I ask.

"Eight hundred and twenty!"

"How many are coming over?" I ask, catching my breath.

"Three. We don't have big enough pots. We need more stuff, you know, we just need more stuff."

So Linda's completely obsessed with having enough food and enough pots to make the food for somewhere between three and hundreds of people! That's when I've got to step in and help her. When she sees that she's allowed herself to get totally confused because of worry, and if she puts away any offense she may have when I confront her with the truth, then she will be able to do what needs to be done and have a good time doing it.

The key to overcoming is to not get offended when someone tells you the truth. Or maybe I should say it like this. You're probably going to be offended, but don't stay offended. It's never fun when someone tells you that a weakness is showing. It's like telling the emperor that he's running around with only his underwear on. Nobody likes to hear that kind of truth.

When people are sent by God to help you through issues of worry in your life, you must learn how to put away any offense because your point of offense is your potential point of failure.

If you allow offenses to overshadow and stop what God is trying to do in your life to set you free, then it is doubtful that you will be able to be successful in all He's called you to do. And it's pretty certain that you won't be very happy with your life.

Most people will say to me, "If you see anything in me that needs correction, Pastor, please tell me. I want to know about anything that is hindering me from following the Lord." When I hear this, I know they are sincere, but I also know that when the time comes for me to confront them, they will not be so easygoing about it!

I have found that most people that say that they can be corrected never can be corrected. They say, "You can correct me," but actually mean, "You better never correct me." They really believe that just saying they can be corrected makes them so perfect that they should never be corrected! And the reason they are saying it in the first place is because they are so worried that something might be wrong with them.

TRUTH AND FAITH DISPEL WORRY

Worry, worry, worry. It is so much a part of our lives that we cannot see it. That's why we need other people to bring us to the truth. If we don't bring each other to the truth in love, we will be overwhelmed with worry ourselves. We will worry so much about the fact that the other person is so worried that we will begin to pick at them, criticize them, and finally line up with the accuser of the brethren and come out and accuse them of being a worrywart.

> Brethren, if a man be overtaken in a fault, ye which are spiritual, restore such an one in the spirit of meekness; considering thyself, lest thou also be tempted.
>
> GALATIANS 6:1

Speaking the truth is not taking the sword of the Spirit and chopping off a person's head! There is a huge difference between confronting a brother or sister in love about worrying too much and *accusing* them of worrying too much. The reason people become accusatory is because they are probably worried about the same thing! And the Bible says that the mature believer will recognize this and go to the other believer humbly and with a teachable spirit. Otherwise, they themselves will become obsessed by the same worry.

Worry is contagious if you allow it to be, but so is faith. Instead of allowing the other person's worry to affect you, let your faith affect them. When you tell the truth in love, you also impart your faith that whatever they are worrying about can be overcome by the Word of God. You show them that you have faith that they can be free.

Jesus often did this with people. When Jairus came to Him and asked Him to heal his daughter, Jesus agreed; but He was delayed by a huge crowd and the woman with the issue of blood who was healed when she touched His robe. He stopped to talk to her, and then one of Jairus's servants broke through the crowd to tell him that his daughter had died. Now Jairus has the chance to jump over any worry about his daughter and land in total despair and grief. Jesus stops that from happening with faith.

> But when Jesus heard what had happened, he said to Jairus, "Don't be afraid. Just trust me, and she will be all right."
> LUKE 8:50 NLT

By His Word Jesus turned Jairus from hopelessness and grief to faith. And when you see someone who is overcome with worry, you need to be a faith magnet instead of a fear magnet. Make sure you are magnetized with the right stuff before you try to help someone else!

CUT IT OUT!

After someone tells me the truth, when I see that I have been obsessed with something that worries me, I need to cut that thing out of my life. I need to stop thinking about it and stop talking about it. This is important because obsessive worry kills my faith in God's Word, and it is the truth of God's Word that sets me free from worry.

"Cutting it out" may mean more than not thinking or talking about something. It also could mean not going to certain places, being with certain people, watching certain television shows or movies, or reading certain magazines or books. In other words, there may be some things in my life that are contributing to my worry, and I need to cut them out.

If other people come up to me and ask why I have stopped doing certain things, I tell them that those things contribute to a weakness that I am overcoming. And it is a good thing to let my close friends in the Lord know what I'm going through because then they can help me.

Believers have to be like compassionate monkeys—yes, I said monkeys! At one time or another, monkeys will stop swinging from trees and making noise in order to sit and pick the dirt, fuzz, bugs, and whatever else off of each other. Every now and then one of them will become irritated and pull away, but most of them are smart enough to know that they aren't going to stay clean and healthy without the help of their fellow monkeys. That bad stuff has to be taken off or it will "worry" them later.

If you are so worried about something that you cannot help yourself, ask God to bring you someone who can minister to you. Or, go to the one you feel He is indicating can help you. Then receive the truth from them and cut that thing that's worrying you out of your life. You may have to go through some change and some pain, but it will be worth it in the end.

8

The Spiritual Cure for Panic Attacks

One of the worst things you can experience in life is panic attacks. I used the plural because panic attacks tend to be chronic and can become quite disabling. Anyone who has ever had them will tell you that, and I am someone who has had them. If you've ever been eaten up with fear, you know what I'm talking about. You're so afraid that you're afraid to tell anybody. And when you're not afraid, you're afraid of being afraid.

When you have a panic attack, you think you're going to die. "I'm going to die, Jesus! I'm going to die!" And sometimes it seems like dying would be a step up, because during a panic attack everything in the world seems wrong. Everything looks dark and frightening and dangerous—even when the sun is shining and all the people around you are happy and smiling.

Your heart races and you're not really sure what's happening. You don't know where your life is going, but wherever it is going is just plain scary. You don't want to go outside your home. You are afraid to leave familiar surroundings. You don't want to be around a lot of people, and you pull inside yourself. You want to be alone so you can manage your fear without anyone knowing you have a problem, but you are afraid of being alone.

You will usually have a few people to call for help, but then you're ashamed they know, which makes it worse. When one of your friends shows up at your door, you feel instant relief that help has arrived, and then within minutes you fall back into the dark pit of fear again. All this does is reinforce the worry that your fear cannot be overcome.

PANIC ATTACKS ARE IN THE BIBLE

Panic attacks generally begin with excessive worry about a number of events or activities in your life such as work, school, health, safety, marriage, children—or simply the thought of making it through the day. The truth is that your worries are speaking louder to you than the Word of God, and they are literally choking you to death. Mentally and emotionally you are caught in a destructive pattern, which the Bible describes very clearly in the book of Deuteronomy.

> And among these nations shalt thou find no ease, neither shall the sole of thy foot have rest: but the LORD shall give thee there a trembling heart, and failing of eyes, and sorrow of mind:
> And thy life shall hang in doubt before thee; and thou shalt fear day and night, and shalt have none assurance of thy life:
> In the morning thou shalt say, Would God it were even! and at even thou shalt say, Would God it were morning! for the fear of thine heart wherewith thou shalt fear, and for the sight of thine eyes which thou shalt see.
>
> DEUTERONOMY 28:65-67

These verses in Deuteronomy are part of the passage of Scripture where God tells Israel what will happen to those who do not worship and serve Him with their whole hearts. He was literally describing a panic attack in these verses! From the trembling heart to the sorrowful mind to having no assurance of your life, He lists the symptoms. It is so bad that in the morning you will say, "I wish it was evening," and in the evening you will say, "I wish it was morning." You wish that it was some other time than it is presently because presently you are being eaten up with worry, fear, and anxiety.

Panic attacks cause us to focus on ourselves in an unhealthy way. All we can think about is our safety, comfort, and well being. "Am I going to be alone when I die or alone the rest of my life?" And we make someone stay with us all the time. They can't leave our presence or our life will become a torment. "I don't want to be alone. Don't leave me! Please, don't leave me!" They stay with us, and we are still panicked.

A panic attack is the end of the line when you're dealing with worry. Most people don't actually die from panic attacks, but you feel like you're going to die when you're having one, and over time they can wear down your body to the point where you could literally die of fear. In Luke 21:26 NLT, the Bible tells us, "Men's hearts will fail them from fear of things to come." People will be so worried about what the future holds that their hearts will stop beating! But the Bible tells us that we have nothing to fear no matter what happens.

GOD'S ANSWER TO THE CURSE OF PANIC ATTACKS

For ye have not received the spirit of bondage again to fear; but ye have received the Spirit of adoption, whereby we cry, Abba, Father.

The Spirit itself beareth witness with our spirit, that we are the children of God:

And if children, then heirs; heirs of God, and joint-heirs with Christ; if so be that we suffer with him, that we may be also glorified together.

For I reckon that the sufferings of this present time are not worthy to be compared with the glory which shall be revealed in us.

ROMANS 8:15-18

What did you receive when you were born again? You did not receive bondage to fear. No! You received the Spirit of adoption. The Holy Spirit is also called the Spirit of adoption because He lives in you, floods your soul with God's love for you, and gives you the revelation that you are now God's child. In other words, you are SAFE! That is the reality of being a new creature in Christ Jesus.

Therefore, all of the fear and anxiety and worry that you inherited from your mother and father and grandparents and great-grandparents are now replaced with a new heritage—the heritage of the Lord Jesus Christ. You are a member of your natural family for a moment of time, but you are a member of God's family now and for eternity. How do I know this is true about you? How do YOU know this is true about you? Read Romans 8:15-18 again! That is the Good News. You have been adopted by God, and that is His cure for panic attacks.

As God's adopted child, you are not subject to the bondage of fear anymore. Anything that is holding you back with worry and fear and panic is something that took hold of you before God became your Father and totally changed your reality. That's why Jesus said in Luke 8:21, "My mother and my brethren are these which hear the word of God, and do it." Why did He say that? He said it because of the failures that were inside His own genetic family. He was not born of Joseph; He was the Son of God. And His brothers and sisters were not going to have the DNA of Joseph and Mary; they were going to have the spiritual DNA of God the Father.

Jesus made it clear that His true brothers and sisters didn't just ascribe to the Word of God but also lived the Word of God. You probably have many Christian friends and acquaintances who ascribe to the Bible but don't live according to the Bible. They have never passed any of the tests. Usually, it's because they are just not willing to give it all up for Jesus. And that's too bad because without the Spirit of adoption leading and guiding you, you are going to get really scared! You're going to be in bondage to fear about the future because you don't understand who your Father is and the eternal glory that lives inside you.

Many people have so much fear based on issues passed to them from generations before them. Even believers who have received Jesus and the peace that passes all understanding can get caught up in those worries and fears that they have inherited from parents and grandparents. They need a revelation of adoption. Did you know that by law, when you adopt a child, you can never disinherit that child? When Jesus said that He would never leave us or forsake us, He meant it. He was speaking from the reality that God has adopted us and we are His forever, no matter what happens!

Now let me ask you a question. Has God ever called you His adopted child? Other than telling you that you have the Spirit of adoption, does the Bible ever actually refer to you as God's "adopted" child? Or does the Word of God always call you His son, His daughter, or His child? The point I'm making here is that even in the world parents who adopt children don't introduce them as their adopted children. That would be implying that they were third-class citizens, not as important, and not as loved. The truth is, adopted children are just as much their children as if they were their naturally born children. Legally, they could disinherit their natural children, but they can never disinherit their adopted children.

God never said that to you either. He never said, "Oh, this is My adopted child. This is the child that just comes to Me through Jesus." No, He said, "This is My son. This is My daughter." Full rights. Joint heir with Jesus Christ. Accepted in the Beloved. Everything that Jesus has is now yours.

You are of God, little children, and have overcome them, because He who is in you is greater than he who is in the world.

1 JOHN 4:4 NKJV

You're not *going* to overcome them. You're not *maybe going* to overcome them. The Bible says, "You *have* overcome them." It's past tense. You have already overcome panic attacks because you are God's child. You have been adopted into His family through the blood of Jesus, and your new position and status as God's child mean that the enemy is completely under your feet.

WALKING IT OUT

Now you're probably asking, "Then why in the world am I not seeing the victory in these areas? Why am I still struggling with worry and fear and panic?" The answer is probably in your own conversation. If you are like me, you may know that you are God's child but you are not thinking, speaking, and acting like it.

In my case, I would read in the Bible that I was God's child and then go out and talk about all my worries and fears. I kept thinking about them, meditating on them, and then that was all I could talk about. I had to come to the point where I refused to think about them. I had to cast those thoughts down and take them captive (see 2 Corinthians 10:3) and then replace them with the truth of God's Word. When I started doing that, I began to stop talking my worries and fears and instead began to speak God's Word about my life.

> *A good man out of the good treasure of his heart bringeth forth that which is good; and an evil man out of the evil treasure of his heart bringeth forth that which is evil: for of the abundance of the heart his mouth speaketh.*
>
> LUKE 6:45

Jesus said that our mouth is going to speak what's in our heart, and that described the sum total of my actions. When I filled my head and heart with God's Word, I began to think, speak, and act like God's child instead of the old man who was lost in his worries and fears. I began to live from the reality that I am God's child now. I am safe.

You are of God and have overcome every worry and every fear, whether that is sickness, poverty, or your family falling apart. I'm not just trying to peddle an idea here. What I'm telling you is that you are God's child and it's just a matter of time before your worry and fear subside and then fade away. Even the demons that Jesus cast out of the madman of Gadera in Matthew 8:29 said to Him, "What have we to do with thee, Jesus, thou Son of God? art thou come hither to torment us before the time?"

Panic attacks have a time. It is just a matter of time before they are completely defeated in your life. Once you get the revelation that you are God's adopted child, that you are safe, that all the worries and fears that have held you in bondage are in the past and you can lay them to rest with the old man because all things have become new; then you will begin to think and speak and act from that truth instead of from your worry and fear. It is only a matter of time before you wake up one day and realize that it has been a long time since you worried about something that used to take up so much of your thought and conversation.

You can overcome panic attacks if you will dedicate yourself to think and meditate on God's Word instead of what you're afraid of. How do I know this? I know this because I experienced it; but more importantly, I know this because God's Word says it. You are God's child and have the full inheritance of peace and authority over every enemy that comes with that position.

Walking it out is something you must choose to do yourself, but you never walk it out by yourself. God is always there. You are His child, and His Holy Spirit lives inside you to remind you that He is your loving Father.

9

Attacking Panic Attacks

When I was having panic attacks it was one of the most miserable times of my life. It was like living in hell while everyone around me was having a normal, wonderful life. I couldn't eat or sleep, and the world was a dark, frightening place. Everything scared me. Worry was literally choking the life out of me.

I would like to say that getting born again solved all my problems and I never had another panic attack after that, but that wasn't the case. I experienced panic attacks again after I was saved. At first, I was completely shocked and confused. But then I began to attack them with God's Word. And the Holy Spirit, our Comforter and Teacher, gave me several principles to defeat them.

CHOOSE FAITH

Attacking panic attacks means you must choose to become a person of faith instead of fear. Choose! Life is a series of choices, and you can choose faith over fear. In 1 John 5:4, the Bible tells us, "Whatsoever is born of God overcomes the world and this is the victory that overcomes the world, even our faith." If you are born of God and Jesus is your Lord and Savior, then you are a person of faith. And Romans 10:17 tells you how to increase and build up your faith. "So then faith comes by hearing and hearing by the Word of God."

What are you listening to? Whatever you listen to is what you are going to produce. Whoever is born of God overcomes the world by their faith, which comes by *hearing,* and *hearing,* and *hearing* the Word of God. Faith comes, increases, and is strengthened by hearing God's Word. You cannot just declare you are a person of faith; you must continually hear the Word of God to be a person of faith.

In 2 Corinthians 5:7 the Bible tells us that we walk by faith and not by sight. Here again we have a choice. I choose not to walk by my feelings. I choose not to walk by the way things look. I choose to walk by what God says. In the old days if someone came up to that old man that used to be Robb Thompson and asked him how he was doing, he would say, "Well, I'm okay under the circumstances." Now I know from the Word of God that circumstances are only a circle I'm standing in, and I have authority over them. I am not under them anymore. My faith and trust in God and His Word put me over them. They are subject to change because in Romans 8:28 He tells me that He works everything to my good. No matter how bad it looks, it will get better.

I remember the day I walked out of the Presbyterian Church free from fear and panic. Those people were so nice to let me take my lunchtime in the basement of their church, where I could confess the Word over my life. I had decided that 2 Corinthians 5:7 was my verse. I can't tell you how many times I said, "I walk by faith and not by sight." Over and over and over again until BOOM! Just like that, I knew that I walked by faith.

When I left the church that day, I wasn't struggling anymore. I had heard it and heard it and agreed with it and agreed with it until faith grew big in me and I was defined by faith. You see, Jesus, the Living Word, is the author and finisher of our faith. Faith can be felt. Faith can be known. And once you know Him, you know you are living in faith and fear can no longer dominate you. When fear comes to call, your faith shuts it down.

> *Now faith is the substance of things hoped for, the evidence of things not seen.*
>
> HEBREWS 11:1

Faith is substance and evidence. Faith is not some type of mystical thing. You know when you are walking in faith in any area of life—you know it. Avoiding an issue does not mean you're walking in faith. That means you're walking in worry, fear, anxiety, and panic. When I had panic attacks, I did everything I could to avoid a problem. I came out of the panic attacks because I attacked my problems with God's Word. I chose faith!

When I attacked my worries with faith, I found they had no substance. They were based on lies and what might happen. Faith is based on God's Word and is the substance of things hoped for and the evidence of things not seen yet. Faith in God and His Word was key to my deliverance from panic attacks.

My feelings didn't change for a while, but I began to act like the Word was true instead of acting like my fears were true. Hearing the Word of God increased my faith in the deliverance I was hoping for and beginning to experience.

> *What doth it profit, my brethren, though a man say he hath faith, and have not works? can faith save him?*
>
> JAMES 2:14

Faith has evidence! The evidence is the works you do in response to God's Word. There's nothing wrong with demanding evidence. You can't put a man in jail without evidence, and you can't bless a man without evidence. There is no profit—no evidence—if a person says they have faith but they do nothing with it.

> *If a brother or sister be naked, and destitute of daily food,*
>
> *And one of you say unto them, Depart in peace, be ye warmed and filled; notwithstanding ye give them not those things which are needful to the body; what doth it profit?*
>
> *Even so faith, if it hath not works, is dead, being alone.*
>
> JAMES 2:15-17

Without corresponding acts of faith, your faith is dead and alone. You cannot build up your faith with God's Word and not express your faith, because when you express your faith it is alive. If you never express it and just keep it to yourself, it dies because it is alone. Faith is Jesus touching others through you. Faith is saying to another human being that Jesus loves them.

> *Yea, a man may say, Thou hast faith, and I have works: show me thy faith without thy works, and I will show thee my faith by my works.*
>
> *Thou believest that there is one God; thou doest well: the devils also believe, and tremble.*
>
> *But wilt thou know, O vain man, that faith without works is dead?*
>
> JAMES 2:18-20

The Word of God tells me that if I believe that I am free from the worries that have no substance, then I must act upon the word of faith that does have substance. If I believe that I am free from the worry, the fear, the anxiety, and the panic attacks, then I have to act like it. I can't say that I believe I'm free in Jesus' name and then start freaking out! The Word brings faith, and the substance of faith enables me to produce works of faith. As a result, my faith grows because it is not dead and alone. I have acted on it, and my faith is alive and profitable for me and for others.

As a child of God, I have the victory which overcomes the world, which is my faith. The victory comes through the avenue of faith; it doesn't come through the avenue of feelings. Victory comes to me because I believe what He did for me; it doesn't come because I'm a nice person or bad things aren't happening to me. Victory comes because I believe God's Word, I speak what I believe, and I act upon what I believe. I choose faith!

BELIEVE AND RECEIVE GOD'S WORD

To attack panic attacks, we must choose to believe that what God's Word says about us is the truth and receive it into our lives. We must choose to believe that what God says in His Word about us is absolutely true. No one can talk us out of it, no circumstances can press it out of us, and nothing we see or hear or experience will make us budge from what God's Word says.

If God said that something belongs to me, then it's mine. Nothing you say can talk me out of it, and nothing you do can steal it from me because God said it was His will and His Word on the matter. I must believe and then receive everything He says is mine. I must own it. For example, if God put it in Linda's heart and my heart that it was time for us to buy a house, we must first believe that what He says is true. It is His will for us to have a new home. So we choose to believe this.

Then we act in faith and do everything we know to do in the natural to see the full manifestation of God's will in our lives. But everything we try to do fails. What are we doing wrong? We can't figure out why we can't get the job done.

The problem is that we have never received the house and called it ours. We continue to confess and pray, "Lord, this is Your house. This house belongs to You, Lord. Thank You for giving us Your house, Lord." Linda and I have to receive what

God said He's already given us before we can give it back to Him. He is trying to give us the house, but we just keep telling Him that it is His! We can only dedicate that house to Him and give it back to Him if it is ours. We must believe AND receive.

In attacking panic attacks, you must believe that God's Word is true and then fully receive the truth into your life. Believe it, receive it, and act on it.

> *Sanctify them through thy truth: thy word is truth.*
>
> JOHN 17:17

We must understand that the Word of God is *the* truth; it is not *a* truth. A truth is temporary and subject to change; *the* truth is the same yesterday, today, and forever. A truth is: Today I feel good; yesterday I felt bad. The truth is: "Whatsoever is born of God overcomes the world and this is the victory that overcomes the world, even our faith" (1 John 5:4). As a child of God my faith overcomes whatever adversity the world throws at me.

> *Fight the good fight of faith, lay hold on eternal life, whereunto thou art also called, and hast professed a good profession before many witnesses.*
>
> 1 TIMOTHY 6:12

The Word of God says faith is a fight, but it is also called a "good fight." The reason it is called a good fight is because you win! But remember this: you cannot decide not to fight; you must fight. You must choose to fight to believe and receive God's Word about you. Every believer is called to fight because every believer lives in dead flesh, a fallen world, and contends with Satan and his demons. You may not have someone else's problem, but you have your own problems.

In order to "lay hold on eternal life," you must fight. Now let me explain something about eternal life. Eternal life does not mean long life; eternal life is a quality of life. Eternal does not just mean forever; it also means the quality of life, the abundant life that Jesus died to give you. Eternal life has within it your health, your prosperity, your safety, your peace, your love, your joy, and your ability to overcome sin. Eternal life enables you to honor and fulfill your commitments. And it has within it your freedom from worry, fear, anxiety, and panic attacks. Eternal life was given to you so that you can walk free in every area of life, but as 1 Timothy 6:12 says, you must fight the good fight of faith to lay hold of it.

> I tell you the truth, whoever hears my Word and believes him who sent me has eternal life and will not be condemned; he has crossed over from death to life.
>
> JOHN 5:24 NIV

People get confused over this verse because they don't understand that eternal life is the quality of life that is made available to us through Jesus Christ. It was given to them at the new birth, but they have to fight to experience it. They must believe that they have it and then receive it.

The devil comes to us with every symptom and temptation and trial under the sun to convince us that we do not have eternal life. Anything we have through being in Christ we must fight for. We must lay hold on eternal, abundant life by fighting the good fight of faith.

Let's say you have a hundred million dollars in the bank. To keep your money from being stolen and in order to withdraw the money from the account, the signature on the withdrawal slip has to match the signature of the one who deposited the money. In this case, faith put eternal life in the bank and only faith can withdraw eternal life from the bank. You must fight the good fight of faith to make a withdrawal of eternal life.

You say, "But God loves everybody. He's merciful. He gives to all of us regardless of what we say or do." Really, that's just wanting all the blessings of God without hearing and obeying His Word. You can't live the abundant life just because you want it. You must fight the good fight of faith to lay hold on it. When you lay hold on it through faith, the bank vault opens because faith is what releases eternal life into your life. Sometimes it is the faith of someone else, but most of the time it is your faith in God and His Word that receives eternal life— the eternal life that overcomes panic attacks!

Some things seem to come fairly easy by faith, and some things come only through a pretty tough fight. But all of them come! And it doesn't matter to me how long it takes for me to lay hold on eternal life and overcome panic attacks because I'm going to overcome. I have chosen to believe that God's Word is true. Everything He says about me is true and I receive it into my life. Everything He has given me is mine and I receive it.

KNOW WHO YOU ARE IN CHRIST

To attack panic attacks you must recognize and understand the truth that you are a new creature in Christ Jesus. The Bible says in 2 Corinthians 5:17 that when you are born again you are a new creature in Christ Jesus, that all the old things have passed away and everything in your life is new. Essentially, you can't hold anything against yourself. You can't condemn yourself for anything in your past because God has forgiven you. You can't be ashamed of anything in your past because God has made you clean, washed you white as snow.

One of the greatest challenges to being free from the worries of life is that we condemn ourselves, pick on ourselves, judge ourselves, and put ourselves down. We are always worried about making a mistake, doing something wrong, messing up, or being just plain foolish. We are continually bringing up and thinking about all the things we did wrong in our past, meditating on these things, and when we do that we fortify just what God's Word tells us to get rid of. That's why we must recognize that we are a new creature and all these things are passed away.

You are a new creature. You are new! You see yourself new. You do not hold anything against yourself anymore because God doesn't hold anything against you anymore. Your past started at the cross. That's your past. You no longer have a past with a long list of good deeds and bad deeds, godly thoughts and sinful thoughts.

> *Jesus blotted out the handwriting of ordinances that were against us which were contrary to us and took them out of the way, nailing those things to the cross.*
>
> COLOSSIANS 2:14

Jesus nailed every sin you have ever committed to the cross. He blotted them out! Everything you ever thought or did that was contrary or opposed to God's law was taken out of the way so you could be free of sin and be reunited with God. When you really get a revelation of being a new creature in Christ Jesus, when you see that all your worries and panic attacks are nailed to the cross, then you will begin to walk in the freedom Jesus purchased for you with His blood.

Understanding and meditating about how you are a new creature helps you to stop thinking about all the things that worried you in the past. Like Job, the more you worry and panic, the more you become bound by them. They come upon you. The things that you fear come closer to you the more you think about them. You attack that destructive pattern when you meditate in God's Word and believe what He says about you, that you are brand new in Christ Jesus.

HAVE NO FEAR BECAUSE GOD IS GREATER

To attack panic attacks you must recognize that in Christ Jesus you have nothing to fear because He is greater than any worry, fear, anxiety, or panic attack. I like what Franklin Roosevelt said, that we have nothing to fear but fear itself. Fear takes on all types of shapes and sizes. It takes on lies and has very little truth in it. But remember this: all fear has a little truth. Very little. Fear is sticking a flashlight under a mouse to make him look like a monster. Yes, there is a rodent in the room, but it is so small and so easy to overcome in reality.

A panic attack becomes like Goliath—loud, arrogant, cocky, huge, strong, and constantly declaring that you are a weak wimp. But what happened to Goliath? A little guy named David came along and knew the truth—the whole truth. He saw that the giant was big, muscular, and a well-trained warrior; but he also knew that the God of Israel was far greater. All David had to do was take the rock of God's Word and sling it at Goliath to bring the giant down.

You might be saying right now, "You don't know what's going on in my life. You can't imagine the stuff that I'm fighting, the things that the devil is saying to me day in and day out." Yes I do! I know what the devil tells you. You aren't going to make it. You're going to die. You're going to be a failure. Your business is going to go down the tubes. You're going to lose your job. Your marriage is miserable and no good, and your kids are probably on drugs or will be on drugs.

The devil tells the same lies to everybody. I'm afraid my husband is cheating on me. I'm afraid my wife just isn't doing right by the kids. I'm afraid. I'm afraid. I'm afraid. The truth is, the devil never told you one good thing, and Jesus told us never to forget that the devil is a liar and the father of all lies. So why are you listening to him? He can't tell the whole truth; he can only tell you part of the truth—the ugly, scary, challenging part—that is nothing compared to the power of God.

The reason the devil tries to get you bound up in a panic attack over everything you're worried about is to incapacitate you. He knows you are a new creature in Christ Jesus and that you have been given authority over him and his demons by God through the blood and name of Jesus. He knows that if you start thinking and meditating about who you really are as the adopted child of God Almighty instead of thinking and meditating about your past and all the worries, fears, and anxieties you had in your past that you will crush him like a bug!

It is vital that you know the truth and believe the truth and act on the truth that you have nothing to fear in Christ Jesus because God is so much greater than anything you will ever face in life. But the devil always introduces one particular word to get us to doubt and worry and eventually get taken out by a panic attack. That is the word "maybe." Maybe God will hear your prayer and maybe He won't. Maybe He will deliver you and maybe He won't. Maybe His Word is true and maybe it isn't. Maybe it's true for some but not for you.

The devil came to me one night and said, "Maybe you are going to die this time. Maybe you are going to die tonight."

I just told him, "Some night I will die, but not tonight. When I'm done with what God has called me to do, then I'm willing to go. I don't want to stay fifteen seconds longer. But not tonight." I said this and went to sleep peacefully because in Christ Jesus I had nothing to fear. My life was in God's hands, not the devil's.

The LORD is on my side; I will not fear: what can man do unto me?

PSALM 118:6

Because the Lord is on my side, I have nothing to fear from the devil and his demons, from the world, or from my own stinking flesh. I do not have to be worried about what another human being can do to me. I do not have to be worried about sinning tomorrow. I do not have to be worried about having a panic attack when something catastrophic happens because I know that God will be there with me, fighting for me, comforting me, meeting all my needs, giving me wisdom and courage, and watching over everything that concerns me because I am His child. He's already decided that He is for me and not against me.

God has already made the decision about you; He is on your side. You don't need to be afraid. What do you think might happen? Whatever happens, God is on your side and you have nothing to fear. Just believe what God says about you and how He says your life is going to go. Do not believe or think on the lies and half-truths the devil tells you. And how can you do this? By meditating in His Word instead of meditating on the devil's lies. And that brings us to the next point.

THINK ON THE RIGHT THINGS

To attack panic attacks, you must think on the right things. What have you been thinking about? What have you been allowing to roll over in your head, in your mind, in your brain? What kind of things do you spend your time meditating on and pondering about? Do you realize that depression consists of a series of negative thoughts? That's all depression is. It's just one negative thought after another.

I believe the reason most people are not diagnosed as depressed is because they have a negative thought and then they have an okay thought to cancel out the negative one. The medical world teaches us that one negative thought needs to have at least seven positive thoughts to counteract one negative thought. The point is that we can stop depression and we can stop panic attacks by doing what the Bible tells us to do.

> *Casting down imaginations, and every high thing that exalteth itself against the knowledge of God, and bringing into captivity every thought to the obedience of Christ.*
>
> 2 CORINTHIANS 10:5

Whenever a negative thought occurs, cast it down and immediately begin meditating on what God's Word says. That is how you attack panic attacks: by stopping the destructive thinking pattern and establishing a godly thinking pattern in its place.

Everyone has weaknesses and faults. Some people can't stop eating sweets. Once they eat a brownie, they want a hot fudge sundae and then cheesecake and then ice cream, and on and on. They can hardly wait to get to another meal. Their thoughts are consumed with what they have in the kitchen, what they want to go out and get at the drive-thru, or what they need to pick up at the grocery store. Weaknesses and faults turn our lives backwards. They live to eat instead of eating to live.

Only by meditating in the Word of God can you turn your life around and go forward instead of backwards. In order to change your course of living to eat to eating to live, you must meditate on God's Word day and night. And the same goes for panic attacks and all the worries that you battle. The Bible tells us in Psalm 119:130 that when God's Word enters our mind and heart it brings light. There is nothing darker than a panic attack, but we can turn that around and dispel that darkness by thinking and meditating on the Word of God. We can literally turn on the light of eternal life inside our soul by thinking God's Word instead of all the worries that make up a panic attack.

Whenever I back off on my meditation of the Word of God, fear attempts to return. It is only the meditation of the Word of God that causes it to leave and stay away. One of the greatest things in my life is that now I understand what the apostle Paul meant when he said that he gloried in his infirmities.

> *And lest I should be exalted above measure through the abundance of the revelations, there was given to me a thorn in the flesh, the messenger of Satan to buffet me, lest I should be exalted above measure.*
>
> *For this thing I besought the Lord thrice, that it might depart from me.*
>
> *And he said unto me, My grace is sufficient for thee: for my strength is made perfect in weakness. Most gladly therefore will I rather glory in my infirmities, that the power of Christ may rest upon me.*
>
> *Therefore I take pleasure in infirmities, in reproaches, in necessities, in persecutions, in distresses for Christ's sake: for when I am weak, then am I strong.*
>
> 2 CORINTHIANS 12:7-10

Paul asked God to take away the thorn in the flesh he was continuously battling, but God said that His grace was sufficient for Paul to walk in victory in that area of his life if he would just allow God's strength to empower him in his weakness. This is incredible! When we are weak, He fills us with His strength. That means that when we worry and start to feel a panic attack coming on, we can turn to Him—knowing that He is on our side—and we will be filled more and more with His strength. We can rejoice at every worry that attacks our mind because we know it is just another opportunity to get more of God's love, power, and wisdom operating in our lives!

Your infirmities, your worries—even your tendency toward panic attacks—drive you back to God. You can't veer too far away because the farther away you veer, the weirder you get. When you walk away from Jesus the panic attacks come back stronger; but when you stay close to Him and walk in His Word, you can keep them away from you. You must always remember what your weaknesses and infirmities are, but at the same time remember that God gave you the anecdote for them!

One important point I want to mention while we're on this subject has to do with who and what you listen to. When you are fighting a battle against something like panic attacks, you can't afford to be around people who are constantly negative and reinforce destructive thinking patterns. You can't afford to watch television shows and movies or play video games that introduce thoughts of worry and fear. These things are hostile toward God's Word. Instead of strengthening your faith in God—who is on your side and wants you to be healthy and whole—they strengthen your worries and fears and anxieties. And that leads to panic attacks. The Bible tells us to think on good stuff, and it's a lot easier to do that when we hang around people and things that encourage us to think on the right things.

> *Finally, brethren, whatsoever things are true, whatsoever things are honest, whatsoever things are just, whatsoever things are pure, whatsoever things are lovely, whatsoever things are of good report; if there be any virtue, and if there be any praise, think on these things.*
>
> PHILIPPIANS 4:8

SPEAK GOD'S WORD

To attack panic attacks you must speak God's Word to them. Your declaration will defeat them. Not only must you think God's Word, but you must also speak His Word to cut off all the lies of the devil and break the power of panic attacks in your life.

> *Thou art snared with the words of thy mouth, thou art taken with the words of thy mouth.*

PROVERBS 6:2

This verse has absolutely revolutionized my life. Usually, when we think of this particular verse, we think of it from the perspective of negativity, that we need to stop saying negative words. But then I started to think about snares. We're caught, can't get away, encased, trapped, and the door is shut on us by our words. We are snared by the words of our mouths. So if we are snared with the words of our mouths, then the words of our mouths are the things that will absolutely govern our lives. That means we can speak God's Word and be snared, caught, encased, trapped, and totally held captive by God!

You are snared by God's Word when you speak it. You are taken by God's Word when you speak it. We can use this principle to our advantage as children of God. We can turn it around and be snared and captured by God's Word. We can become a prisoner to God's Word instead of being a prisoner to the worries and fears of panic attacks.

> *Depression in the heart of man causes him to stoop, but a good word will make him glad.*

PROVERBS 12:25

When we think and meditate on God's Word, we are receiving the good word that will make us glad. And then when we speak that good word over ourselves and our lives, we bring gladness to our environment and to everyone around us. The devil hates it when we speak God's truth over our situations, and panic attacks are no exception. The Bible says that the Word of God is the sword of the Spirit (see Eph. 6:17), and we must speak His Word to drive panic attacks and all those worrisome thoughts out of our lives.

AGREE WITH SOMEONE

To attack panic attacks it is helpful to find another believer who can truly agree with you. You don't need somebody telling you that they're thinking about agreeing with you. You need solid agreement. And you don't need a mob to agree. You just need one believer who is full of faith like you are. In Matthew 18:19 Jesus said, "If any two of you shall agree as touching anything that they shall ask it shall be done for them by the Father who is in heaven."

Now I want you to think about this from a negative perspective for a moment. In Genesis, chapter 11, it gives us the story of the Tower of Babel. The Tower of Babel is where all the nations of the world came together, and they were in agreement because they all spoke the same language.

> And the LORD said, Behold, the people is one, and they have all one language; and this they begin to do: and now nothing will be restrained from them, which they have imagined to do.
>
> Go to, let us go down, and there confound their language, that they may not understand one another's speech.
>
> GENESIS 11:6,7

The word "confound" doesn't mean that one minute they were talking in Portuguese and the next minute they were talking Pig Latin. Every nation wasn't speaking Hebrew and then suddenly each nation was speaking a different language like Irish or Spanish. That's not what happened. The word "confound" means to make something vague.[1] All of a sudden when somebody from one nation told someone from another nation to come over to their house, all the other person heard was, "Come over to my crib."

God confounded their languages or made them vague and unable to understand clearly to keep the people from staying in agreement. They could do anything if they were in agreement, including serving themselves and other gods instead of God. It was His mercy that confounded their languages so that their agreement could not be maintained. The Bible says that they could not build the Tower of Babel any longer because they could not understand what each other was saying; therefore, they could not agree about anything.

If we turn this principle around to the positive, believers have great power and authority when they agree in prayer according to God's Word and will. But if we are not specific and clear—if we are vague—then other believers cannot truly agree with us. We need *real* agreement. How can we agree to an unspoken request? It's impossible. It doesn't work, does it? Because we cannot agree over something that is not clearly and specifically stated.

I want specifics because God's Word is specific. And I want someone to agree with me who will stick to the agreement and not change their mind and confession two days later because the going gets tough. That means that there is a commitment that they will not break.

How does a person come out of an agreement? Very simply, they quit believing and confessing what they agreed to. It's no longer important to them, it's not something that they can stick with, or they have let the cares of life or the lies of the devil talk them out of it. But even then, if they have a good heart and have just been overtaken with a fault for a moment, we can help them come back into agreement with us.

> *Two are better than one; because they have a good reward for their labour.*
>
> *For if they fall, the one will lift up his fellow: but woe to him that is alone when he falleth; for he hath not another to help him up.*
>
> *Again, if two lie together, then they have heat: but how can one be warm alone?*
>
> *And if one prevail against him, two shall withstand him; and a threefold cord is not quickly broken.*
>
> ECCLESIASTES 4:9-12

The third person in the "threefold cord" is God! When you and I agree with God's Word, then He will become part of our agreement. In Philippians 1:7-8, the Bible talks about partnership.

> *It is right that I should feel as I do about all of you, for you have a very special place in my heart. We have shared together the blessings of God, both when I was in prison and when I was out, defending the truth and telling others the Good News.*
>
> *God knows how much I love you and long for you with the tender compassion of Christ Jesus.*
>
> PHILIPPIANS 1:7,8

When you are attacking panic attacks it's good to have somebody partner with you in prayer. You've got to link with someone who can agree with you, someone who cares about you, someone who has you in their heart. Someone who has you in their heart will not abandon you or the agreement for victory that you have made.

You must leave independence and walk before God in interdependence with other believers. None of us can fulfill our callings or walk right with God by ourselves. We need each other. In the fight against panic attacks, you may also need a Christian counselor or Christian physician, not only to help you expose the lies and strategies of the enemy, but also to agree with you for complete deliverance. There is never any shame in asking for help!

The devil tries to make us believe that we are weak and stupid if we can't do everything by ourselves. As usual, that is a lie! Remember the first two commandments? Love God and love your neighbor as yourself. You can't do that alone. God puts other believers in our lives because if any two of us shall agree upon this earth as touching anything that we'll ask in Jesus' name and according to His will, it shall be done for us by the Father who is in heaven. The devil knows this truth and tries to keep you from walking in it. He knows that when you do, you will defeat any attack he wields against you, including panic attacks.

1 0

Worry and Relationships

We have seen how important relationships are in the body of Christ, especially when we are dealing with defeating worry and fear. That's why Satan does everything he can to destroy good, godly relationships. His world is charged with negativity, distrust, selfishness, and suspicion. Unfortunately, the church is often influenced more by the world than the Bible. If I were to go out and do ten great and wonderful things and then do one bad thing, what would the church be talking about? They would all be buzzing about how I had missed God or messed up.

The world is going in a negative direction, and if we're going in a positive direction we are swimming upstream. Look at the amount of effort that a salmon has to give in order to swim upstream and fulfill his mission before his death. Like salmon, it takes a tremendous amount of effort for believers to stay positive, full of faith, and trusting God for every blessing in life. And this is something that cannot be done alone.

In order to go beyond this place of just maintaining to a place where we're possessing, in order to change the current of the stream, we must have enough salmon swimming upstream to change it. Together we must get rid of worry and fear, which is the opposite of faith, to possess the stream instead of continually fighting against it.

We must possess our future, not just try to maintain where we are right now. We've got to go beyond making do and take ground. We've got to go farther tomorrow than we traveled today. And the only way we can do that is to stop worrying, trust God, and move forward together.

I trust God by believing and doing what He's written in the pages of His Book. And I look for people to connect with who do the same. Don't tell me, "God told me," and then go out and do something that isn't in the pages of the Book! But if you live according to the pages and your life shows the fruit of it, then I want to network with you. I want to know what God's telling you and where you're going and how I can help you get there.

BE OF ONE MIND—WORRY FREE

There are so many Scriptures exhorting us to be of one mind that it staggers me. You know why it staggers me? Because most believers in the body of Christ don't believe it's possible for all believers to be of one mind. I don't know about you, but I've always heard that we will never agree on everything, and the only way we will ever come into unity as the Bride of Christ is to let the Holy Spirit give us all the same goosebumps at the same time. We make unity some kind of spiritual phenomenon and totally leave out how we think about things. But read some of these Scriptures and see what happens to *your* thinking.

> *Be of the same mind one toward another. Mind not high things, but condescend to men of low estate. Be not wise in your own conceits.*
> ROMANS 12:16

> *Now the God of patience and consolation grant you to be likeminded one toward another according to Christ Jesus:*
> *That ye may with one mind and one mouth glorify God, even the Father of our Lord Jesus Christ.*
> ROMANS 15:5,6

Now I beseech you, brethren, by the name of our Lord Jesus Christ, that ye all speak the same thing, and that there be no divisions among you; but that ye be perfectly joined together in the same mind and in the same judgment.

1 CORINTHIANS 1:10

Finally, brethren, farewell. Be perfect, be of good comfort, be of one mind, live in peace; and the God of love and peace shall be with you.

2 CORINTHIANS 13:11

Only let your conversation be as it becometh the gospel of Christ: that whether I come and see you, or else be absent, I may hear of your affairs, that ye stand fast in one spirit, with one mind striving together for the faith of the gospel.

PHILIPPIANS 1:27

Fulfil ye my joy, that ye be likeminded, having the same love, being of one accord, of one mind.

PHILIPPIANS 2:2

I beseech Euodias, and beseech Syntyche, that they be of the same mind in the Lord.

PHILIPPIANS 4:2

Finally, be ye all of one mind, having compassion one of another, love as brethren, be pitiful, be courteous.

1 PETER 3:8

Forasmuch then as Christ hath suffered for us in the flesh, arm yourselves likewise with the same mind: for he that hath suffered in the flesh hath ceased from sin.

1 PETER 4:1

It's interesting that the enemies of Christ who serve the beast in the book of Revelation are also of one mind.

These have one mind, and shall give their power and strength unto the beast.

REVELATION 17:13

Two things are certain from reading these Scriptures: 1) God wants His body to be of one mind; and 2) It must be possible for the body of Christ to be of one mind. Why? God also knows the power and authority we can walk in when we come into likeminded unity under Him.

These verses also give us specific keys to having one mind. In Romans 12:16 NIV it says, "Live in harmony with one another. Do not be proud, but be willing to associate with people of low position. Do not be conceited." This verse and the others above are talking about our *attitude* toward one another. We are to have the same attitude of love and respect toward each other. So the Bible is not talking about agreeing on every doctrine. What the Holy Spirit is telling us is that we must treat each other with a holy attitude of honor, that no one is more important than another.

What does that have to do with getting rid of worry? In relationships we tend to worry about whether we are as important, as gifted, and as valuable to God as other believers. Remember when Jesus was walking with Peter on the beach after His resurrection, telling Peter how he would live and die for Him? Peter doesn't even stop to react to what Jesus tells him about his life, but looks over to see John and asks, "What about him?" Peter has not got it yet! He is so insecure about his position in the body of Christ, so concerned that he be as important or more important than John. (See John 21:15-22.)

Second Corinthians 10:12 tells us clearly that we are not wise if we compare ourselves among ourselves. All this does is stir up strife, division, envy, and all-out jealousy. That is why the Word of God exhorts us again and again to be "of one mind," or to have the same attitude toward one another. We are simply to love, respect, and honor each other as God does all of us. If we do this, then we won't worry about whether we're better or worse than other believers; we'll simply glorify God.

The Bible gives us an example of what not to do.

> For it hath been declared unto me of you, my brethren, by them which are of the house of Chloe, that there are contentions among you.
>
> Now this I say, that every one of you saith, I am of Paul; and I of Apollos; and I of Cephas; and I of Christ.
>
> Is Christ divided? was Paul crucified for you? or were ye baptized in the name of Paul?
>
> 1 CORINTHIANS 1:11-13

This is a picture of the church today. There are contentions among us, and we call them denominations and movements. I could spend several chapters listing and describing the different groups in the body of Christ, who their leaders are, and all the things they disagree about. Paul answers this with, "Is Christ divided?" These verses of Scripture tells us that the only thing that is going to bring the body of Christ together is for all believers to be of one mind.

Now don't misunderstand me. Doctrine is important, especially when it comes to the birth, life, death, and resurrection of Jesus Christ. The fundamental truths—He was born of a virgin (God being His Father), led a sinless life, shed His innocent blood to pay the price for our sin and fulfill the Law, was resurrected from the dead to give us the new birth, and we must be born again by the Holy Spirit to be saved—are not negotiable. But most Christian denominations and movements agree on these fundamental doctrines and allow the enemy to get them worried and uptight about the less important places in the Word where we disagree.

First Peter 4:1 really sums up this whole issue. We are to arm ourselves with the same mind that Jesus had when He died on the cross for us. We are to lay down our lives—stop worrying about our doctrines and traditions that have nothing to do with whether we're saved or not—and love one another as He loved us and continues to love us. Then we can enjoy the comfort and compassion we give to one another and truly glorify God in this world.

AVOID WORRY IN YOUR MARRIAGE

Aside from your relationship with Jesus Christ, your relationship with your spouse is the most important in your life. And having a godly marriage where you are likeminded eliminates a lot of worry! There are lots of Christian books about making a marriage work, giving you keys to making your marriage a source of joy instead of misery. These are helpful, but what Linda and I have found to be the most crucial key to keeping worry out of our marriage is sticking to THE Book, the Word of God.

I can't come up to Linda and tell her, "This is what the Holy Spirit told me," and proceed to tell her something that conflicts with what is written in Scripture. So many Christians use the Holy Spirit as an excuse for not knowing what's in the Word, and they get themselves and everyone who follows them in trouble. There are no "extra" and "new" revelations. Everything is contained in God's Word. The only way I know I'm pleasing God is by fulfilling what He's written.

When I understand this, I don't have to be uptight all the time, worrying if I'm being a good husband to Linda. I know I'm supposed to love her as Christ loves the Church. I'm actually able to go to her and say, "Please explain to me how I can love you like Jesus loves the Church. Because that's the responsibility God gave me, I need God to show me and for you to help me. If I have not loved you, please tell me."

> *For a husband is the head of his wife as Christ is the head of his body, the church; he gave his life to be her Savior.*
>
> *Husbands, love your wives, just as Christ loved the church and gave himself up for her.*
>
> EPHESIANS 5:23,25

Linda can then say, 'Well, Ephesians, chapter 5, verses 23 and 25, say that you are to love me like Jesus does and give your life to save me, to take care of me. When you don't go to work, sleep all day, stay up watching TV all night, and expect me to go to work and pay all the bills, you have not loved me like Christ loves the Church. You're not laying your life down for me. You're just laying your body down!" That is concrete. It is right there in Book. And since we are agreed that the Word is the standard for our marriage, then I have no problem getting off the bed and finding a job.

I've seen young women look at their jobless, aimless boyfriends and say, "I know he loves me. I know he'll take care of me and protect me." No, they won't! Look what happened in the Garden. Adam's disobedience to God's Word by not stepping up when the serpent beguiled Eve bankrupt us all. We were all scratching around trying to make a living and trying to feel any kind of good emotion toward each other until Jesus redeemed us! But we can't expect to live in blessing if we don't obey the Word of God. And if your boyfriend isn't obeying the Word now, don't expect him to obey it after you're married. Save yourself a life of worry and marry someone who fears God and obeys His Word.

When we can articulate what the Word of God actually says, then we won't be helpless and hopeless when things aren't going well. If Linda feels like she's not being loved, she has to be able to articulate it so that I can understand why I am not becoming what God wants me to become.

The problem might be that Linda doesn't want to be loved. Do you know there are times when people reject love, when they won't let you near them? There are times when you don't want to be touched and you'll reject love and push people away. You cannot fulfill your call and your mate cannot fulfill theirs if you are pushing each other away. That is serious business!

I can say to my wife, "Linda, God says that you are to let me love you as Christ loves the Church." Again, we are dealing in real truth because it is God's Word. Nobody's wondering or guessing, and we don't have to worry about missing something. If we are offended, we are offended because we don't like what the Word is telling us.

"Well, I don't think that it's real important for me, you know, to love my wife like Christ loves the Church." Really? Then you don't think the Bible is the Word of God and that it means what it says? Maybe you need a little more explanation.

> *Husbands, love your wives, even as Christ also loved the church, and gave himself for it;*
>
> *That he might sanctify and cleanse it with the washing of water by the word,*
>
> *That he might present it to himself a glorious church, not having spot, or wrinkle, or any such thing; but that it should be holy and without blemish.*
>
> *So ought men to love their wives as their own bodies. He that loveth his wife loveth himself.*
>
> *For no man ever yet hated his own flesh; but nourisheth and cherisheth it, even as the Lord the church.*
>
> EPHESIANS 5:25-29

We are not only to love our wives as Jesus loves the Church, but we are to love them the way we love our own bodies and ourselves! This is a big stretch for a lot of us because not many of us love our bodies or ourselves. There is hope, however, because God loves us. When that becomes real on the inside of us, things begin to change for the better.

The way I believe God loves me is the way I will love Linda. The way I believe God takes care of me is the way I will take care of her. If I'm mean to her, then I believe God's mean to me. If I don't love my wife, I don't love myself, and I don't love myself because I don't believe God loves me. Do you see how that works?

When husbands understand this, it takes all the worrying out of being a good husband. All we have to do is remember how much God loves us and all the wonderful things He does for us. Then we can turn around and love our wives and do for them in the same way.

I didn't love myself for so long, and it was hard to be a husband. I was constantly worried, afraid, and insecure about how I was treating Linda, which made it nearly impossible to love her as Jesus loves the Church. But when I started focusing on how much God loved me and began to receive His love for me, then my heart expanded. I could give her more love because I had more love to give.

Husband, what are you going through? Check your heart and see if you have become hardened inside. Check whether or not you are really soft and forgiving and loving. Are you forbearing or overbearing? Are your heart and mind being led by your worries and fears or by God's Word? Are you allowing your heart to be expanded by God's love for you?

Wife, are you worrying about whether your husband is really walking with God the way you want him to? Are you uptight about how much he prays and reads his Bible? Is it a major crisis if he skips church to go hunting or fishing once in awhile? The Bible has something to say to women who worry about these things.

> *Likewise, ye wives, be in subjection to your own husbands; that, if any obey not the word, they also may without the word be won by the conversation of the wives;*
>
> *While they behold your chaste conversation coupled with fear.*
>
> *Whose adorning let it not be that outward adorning of plaiting the hair, and of wearing of gold, or of putting on of apparel;*
>
> *But let it be the hidden man of the heart, in that which is not corruptible, even the ornament of a meek and quiet spirit, which is in the sight of God of great price.*
>
> 1 PETER 3:1-4

There is something really powerful about a woman who respects and submits to her husband without disobeying the Word of God. In other words, if her husband tells her to do something that is against the Word of God, she respectfully tells him she can't because it is against her faith. Then she goes on to actually live her faith in front of him, showing him the love and respect that Jesus has for him. He sees that her heart—that meek and quiet spirit within her—can't be corrupted and she is a beautiful ornament in his life. Not only does this please God, but also it wins him over to obey the Lord.

Women, if you will just live to please God and respect and love your husbands, you will accomplish a lot more godly change in them than constantly nagging and complaining. "You never go to church with me. We never pray together. Why can't we at least go to a couples' Bible study?" Nag. Nag. Nag. And you wonder why he never wants to do anything with you that has to do with God.

Why not go fishing with him some weekend and ask him what's going on in his life? Let him pour out his heart and then encourage him. You can speak the truth in love without quoting chapter and verse! And when he asks you how you got so smart, you can say that it's not your wisdom; it's God's wisdom. If you do the Word and trust God, you will not be worried anymore.

Husbands don't get off the hook either.

> *Likewise, ye husbands, dwell with them according to knowledge, giving honour unto the wife, as unto the weaker vessel, and as being heirs together of the grace of life; that your prayers be not hindered.*

1 PETER 3:7

Husbands are always to remember that their wives are joint-heirs with Jesus Christ; they must honor them as their equals in the sight of God. Women are weaker physically, so they need their husband's protection, but they are not to use that to justify feeling superior and more important than their wives.

I'll tell you how serious God is about husbands treating their wives right. He says that He won't answer our prayers if we don't! You talk about living a life of worry! We men can avoid a lot of worrying and pacing the floor if we treat our wives with honor and love them as God loves them. That doesn't mean we aren't the head of our homes; it means we are secure in who we are in God, and loving our wives gives them the confidence to trust our leadership in the home. Then God can answer our prayers because our home is lined up with His Word. We are in agreement. We are likeminded. And we put our family in position for His blessings when we do things His way.

There is no doubt about the fact that when you conduct your marriage according to God's Word, you can avoid and defeat a lot of worrying that would otherwise lead to major misery in your life. If you want to keep from worrying, I suggest you approach your marriage from the perspective of God's Word instead of your own needs and desires. If you do marriage God's way and love each other the way God loves each of you, you'll reap great joy and a multitude of blessings—and worry will be locked out of your home.

NO WORRIES WITH GODLY FRIENDS

We all need good, godly friends who will stick with us no matter what we're going through. These are believers who understand the true meaning of covenant, who won't desert us when we mess up or when we are under a severe attack. They know all our faults and weaknesses and still love us, pray for us, and stand with us during trials and temptations.

On the other hand, all of us want to be loved and accepted by the people around us. None of us like to be rejected. And we need to understand that being a good, godly friend means sticking with the Word of God even if it means risking a friendship. Some believers think that they have to compromise the Word in order to keep a friendship. They put the friendship before the Word of God thinking they can straighten it all out later. They think that if they compromise now, later on their friend will come to agree with the truth of God's Word because they were so loving and bending. But the exact opposite is true. Ultimately people do not respect someone who doesn't live what they believe.

The truth is, our love is unconditional because we love people out of God's love for us. But the Word of God is not unconditional. The Word of God is what God thinks, how He speaks, and what He does; and there's no room for compromise there. What He says is what He means. Do not bear false witness. If a good friend asks you to lie for him, you have to say no. If you lie for him, not only do you sin against God but also you destroy your witness for Jesus to your friend.

Good, godly friends may mess up, get scared, and ask you to do something that is against the Word of God. But if they are truly good, godly friends, they will be grateful when you refuse to compromise God's Word and point them back to the truth and His faithfulness by doing the right thing.

This is really what loving your neighbor as yourself is all about. We are to worship God in spirit and truth, and I believe we are to love our brothers and sisters—and unbelievers—in the power of the Holy Spirit and the Word of God. The first commandment is directly related to the second commandment. If you don't love God with all your heart, soul, mind, and strength, you will not be able to love your neighbor as yourself—or be a good friend in the Lord.

> *Love worketh no ill to his neighbour: therefore love is the fulfilling of the law.*
>
> ROMANS 13:10

Love fulfills the whole law! This is what Jesus meant when He said that all of the Law and the Prophets could be summed up in the first two commandments: love God and love your neighbor as yourself. You have to walk in love because the Bible tells you to. But in a practical sense, just why is that so important? How does this really work?

The reason God made unconditional love the standard is because He is love. That's who He is and how He operates, and He expects His children to think and act like He does. Therefore, we should walk in love and be His love to everyone we meet and associate with. But God also understands that we are still walking around in this stinky flesh. You put two people—even believers—in a room together, and they are going to disagree about something. Only love can override the disagreement, maintain peace, and sustain unity.

Even the disagreements you don't want are going to come anyway. The devil will make sure of it. Life isn't perfect. All you need to do is know another human being to find that out! If you have anything that involves two people, things are not perfect. Why is that? Because there are two different personalities, two different backgrounds, two different histories of hurt and joy and failure and success, and two different visions of the future. Sometimes there are two people who are simply polar opposites on every subject except that Jesus is their Lord and Savior!

Thank God that His love never fails. We can walk in love with people. It's wonderful. Even if we have friends like Job's. Do you remember what they had to say to him in his darkest days? Instead of trying to build him up by saying, "Listen man, you're going to make it," they said, 'Look Job, you said you believed. If you really believed, how come all this stuff happened to you? Why are you going through such a hard time? Is God really on your side? What have you done that God would do this to you?"

When you go through trials and tribulations like Job did, there are people who can almost convince you that God's not real. Now if I had friends like Job's, I'd want to kick them out of my house and never speak to them again. But God doesn't do things my way! First, He talked to Job about Job's mistakes, and Job had to get himself straightened out before he could deal with anyone else.

> Then Job answered the LORD, and said,
> I know that thou canst do every thing, and that no thought can be withholden from thee.
>
> Who is he that hideth counsel without knowledge? therefore have I uttered that I understood not; things too wonderful for me, which I knew not.

Hear, I beseech thee, and I will speak: I will demand of thee, and declare thou unto me.

I have heard of thee by the hearing of the ear: but now mine eye seeth thee.

Wherefore I abhor myself, and repent in dust and ashes.

JOB 42:1-6

Job finally realized that he had not had a clear understanding of God's greatness and majesty. Through his great suffering he had come to see God more clearly. So he repented of his pride and ignorance. Then God did an amazing thing.

And it was so, that after the LORD had spoken these words unto Job, the LORD said to Eliphaz the Temanite, My wrath is kindled against thee, and against thy two friends: for ye have not spoken of me the thing that is right, as my servant Job hath.

Therefore take unto you now seven bullocks and seven rams, and go to my servant Job, and offer up for yourselves a burnt offering; and my servant Job shall pray for you: for him will I accept: lest I deal with you after your folly, in that ye have not spoken of me the thing which is right, like my servant Job.

So Eliphaz the Temanite and Bildad the Shuhite and Zophar the Naamathite went, and did according as the LORD commanded them: the LORD also accepted Job.

And the LORD turned the captivity of Job, when he prayed for his friends: also the LORD gave Job twice as much as he had before.

JOB 42:7-10

In the end, Job's friends weren't so bad. After all, they also feared and loved the Lord. When He commanded them to repent and offer sacrifices for their "folly," they did it without questioning Him. But the condition on which the Lord would fully restore Job was that he pray for the very friends who had discouraged him during his trial! Verse 10 above says that only when Job prayed for his friends did the Lord turn things around for him, giving him twice as much as he had before all his trials.

What is most obvious here is that God is very serious about friendship. He is a covenant God, and when He looks at friendship, He sees covenant. Covenant means loving someone unconditionally while not compromising God's Word. It means speaking the truth in love. It means being honest without malice. And what happens when we honor God in our friendships? We don't have to worry about them!

There's no getting around the fact that when you conduct your friendships according to God's Word and His Spirit, you cut out all the worry. You will not worry about what they think about you if you do the right thing and love them as God loves them.

TRAIN UP YOUR CHILDREN: NO WORRIES ABOUT YOUR FUTURE

As a husband and father I have to face all my insecurities about representing God to my family and then turn around and intercede to God on behalf of my family. It is an awesome and overwhelming responsibility to be the prophet, priest, and king in my home. To me, being king is probably the most intimidating, the job that I don't like the most. When you're a king, that means you must rule. I don't like to rule because I don't like to be ruled. I have been abused by those who have ruled over me, so ruling wisely is a real challenge to me.

The truth is, none of us will ever rule over any other human being—not to mention our children—if we aren't abiding in God's Word and living it ourselves. Most family counselors and experts will tell you that your children are more impressed by how you live your life in front of them than all the lecturing and preaching you do. They notice how you treat your husband or wife. They observe what kind of friends you have and how you treat them. Their eyes and ears are wide open to whatever your life has to say to them.

- Do you fear and love God and His Word, or do you "hedge" and "bend the rules"?

- Are you active in your church, or do you make excuses not to go all the time?

- Do you have your priorities straight, or do you give all your time to work and little to anything or anyone else?

- When you sin or make a mistake, do you take responsibility and repent, or do you blame someone else and make excuses?

- When someone offends you do you work through it with God and forgive, or do you hold a grudge?

- Do you tithe and give offerings, and are you a wise and generous steward of the rest of what God gives you; or do you find excuses not to give and spend your money without thought or a financial plan?

These are just some of the things our children learn from us. They are not interested in what we say unless our words match our behavior. If they don't see that what we say is what we do, then they will not be interested in what we have to say. James said it like this: faith without corresponding works is dead faith. (See James 2:20,26.)

The Bible says in Proverbs 22:6, "Train up a child in the way he should go: and when he is old, he will not depart from it." "Training" is the big show-and-tell game with children. If you show them then you can tell them. And sometimes we have to really exercise a lot of patience with ourselves and with them to play this game right!

Why is God so interested in how we teach and train our children? Children are His future and our future. And if we want to be free from worry forever, that includes our future. We don't have to worry about our children if we've trained them to love and fear God and His Word, to obey Him and serve Him, and to love others as they love themselves. Jesus told us that if we followed the first two commandments, we would fulfill the whole Law. So if we teach our children to love God and love others then we have no worries about their future or ours.

BEING TRUE ELIMINATES WORRY

In my relationships, I want to know all the time, "Okay, what do I need to do? Tell me what makes you happy with me. What makes you sad with me? Because I want to do the things that make you happy. I want to stay away from the things that make you sad because I want to have a nice day. And more than that, I want you to have a nice day."

This sounds pretty unselfish but it really isn't. I'm not being totally true to my feelings. Part of the reason I'm so concerned about what makes everyone happy is because I want everyone to like me, so I'll be to them what they want me to be to them. That's not being true or honest. And guess what? When you live like this, you are constantly worrying what other people think and feel about you.

Human beings are really funny. We can love someone and treat them like dirt. We can hate someone else and treat them like royalty. That's because we aren't afraid of the people who are closest to us because we know we have their affection. Our spouse, our children, our family—all the people we love most—are the ones we can treat the worst because we know they are bound to us and are supposed to love us no matter what. But we are afraid of the person we don't know very well because they might not like us. So we treat them with incredible kindness and respect in order to keep from being rejected and hurt.

I can't encourage you to have relationships that will give you no worries without encouraging you to be true to yourself in the context of God's Word. That means, be honest about what you believe with God, with yourself, and with your friends and family. Be honest about what's really bothering you and take it to God before taking it out on someone else. Take a good look at whom you really love and trust and who really loves and trusts you. Are you serving and complimenting the ones who really don't love and trust you, the ones you don't really love and trust? Or are you solidly connected with people who are true to themselves and to God's Word, walk in covenant with you, and love you and trust you in spite of yourself?

You might have a problem with whom you allow in your life. If you allow the right people in your life then right things will happen. The right people will realize that they are in your life to help you build it. They're not in your life to destroy it. Proverbs 18:24 NLT says, "There are 'friends' who destroy each other, but a real friend sticks closer than a brother."

There are two types of friends: those who will destroy you if you let them, and those who stick so close to you that they will multiply your life. After you figure out which friends will stick closer than a brother, then you need to understand that you have your part to play also. When one of my ministry friends calls and wants me to come because he's in trouble and he needs me, I've got to get on a plane and go see him. Why? Because he would do the same thing for me. If he sticks closer than a brother then I have to stick closer than a brother.

But I'll tell you something else that is equally as important as getting on that plane. I have to be honest about how I feel about all this. I have to get it straight with God if I resent my friend for asking or if going to see him is going to cost me something I don't want to pay. I want to build him up and not tear him down when I get there. And I also have to make certain it's God's will for me to go. The Holy Spirit might be working something in my friend that I would interfere with. This is what I mean when I say that you've got to be true to God and His Word and who you are in Him.

Someone said once that if you are honest, you never have to worry about what you've said or done in the past. You don't have to worry about "covering your tracks" or coming up with alibis or excuses. The same is true in relationships. If you don't want to worry, it's so simple—although often hard—to do the right thing. Just be honest about what's going on inside you, let God and His Word deal with you, and go on being true to Him and who He made you to be. If you do that today, you won't have to worry about it tomorrow, and your relationships will be full of life and joy.

11

My Testimony:
Freedom From Worry About the Past

This is a faithful saying, and worthy of all acceptation, that Christ Jesus came into the world to save sinners; of whom I am chief.

However for this reason I obtained mercy, that in me first Jesus Christ might shew all longsuffering, as a pattern to those who are going to believe on him for everlasting life.

1 TIMOTHY 1:15,16

The reason I opened with this particular scripture is because this is the way I felt about my life when I got saved. When Jesus Christ came into the world to save sinners, I believed that I was the chiefest among them. When I came to Christ, down inside of me I knew that there was something very wrong between God and me. I had discredited Him, persecuted Him, and mocked Him. I mocked His name. I mocked His memory. I mocked everything about Him. Cursing God had been a sport for me. I enjoyed saying things that would make Christian's ears curl.

After I got saved, I learned that there was someone else who also felt they were the worst sinner Christ died for, and that was the apostle Paul.

PAUL'S TESTIMONY

The apostle Paul probably understood the love and forgiveness of God more than any other believer. He was originally called Saul of Tarsus, which was a Greek city, so of course he spoke Greek. But Paul says in Philippians 3:5 that he was a "Hebrew of the Hebrews." His family probably lived in a Jewish section of Tarsus where they had absolutely nothing to do with the Greeks. This had always been a custom of Jewish people through the centuries. Why? Because it preserved the nation of Israel. They did this to keep themselves pure.

A biblical example of this is found in Genesis, chapter 46, when Jacob (whom God had renamed Israel) moved to Egypt to be reunited with his son Joseph. Joseph told his father to tell Pharaoh that he was a shepherd, knowing the Egyptians despised shepherds and considered them unclean. Because Pharaoh loved Joseph, he told Jacob that his people could settle in the land of Goshen. This would place them away from the Egyptians. Pharaoh didn't know that the children of Israel considered the Egyptians to be unclean!

When the children of Israel entered the land of Goshen, there were approximately seventy of them. When they left Egypt in the Exodus under Moses, they were several million strong. They grew in number and preserved their nation because they were set apart from the Egyptians. When the apostle Paul said that he was a Hebrew of the Hebrews, he was referring to the fact that he and his family were separated from and had remained untainted from the defilements of the world.

Saul was a Pharisee, and the Pharisees were the religious fanatics of the Jewish nation. A male child of the Pharisees memorized the book of Leviticus by the time he was four years old, and on his fourth birthday they would pour honey over the scroll and have him lick it off. This illustrated Psalm 119:103, "How sweet are thy words unto my taste! yea, sweeter than honey to my mouth!"[1]

By the time the boy was twelve years of age, he had memorized the Pentateuch, the first five books of our Bible, which includes Genesis, Exodus, Leviticus, Numbers, and Deuteronomy. Also at twelve, he had his *bar mitzvah*, where he would stand as a man before the Sanhedrin and be drilled with questions about the Law of Moses. And these were not true-and-false questions! They were deep questions that required a thorough understanding of the Scriptures.

After Paul had his *bar mitzvah*, he moved to Jerusalem to study with the rabbi named Gamaliel. Gamaliel was probably the most famous and well-respected rabbi at that time. He gave Saul of Tarsus the best education in Judaism that money could buy. When Saul emerged years later, he was a full-fledged Pharisee of the Pharisees. He was Gamaliel's star pupil and joined the Sanhedrin at a very early age because he was so highly respected by the Jewish leaders in Jerusalem.

The Pharisees were so religious that they had to do everything a little better and a little greater than everyone else. Even the way they dressed indicated that they studied and prayed more than other Jews did. When Saul of Tarsus walked into town with his flowing robes, his prayer shawl, and his phylacteries, the people of Israel knew they were dealing with a heavyweight Pharisee of the Pharisees.

The first time the Bible introduces us to Saul of Tarsus, he is in Jerusalem. The city is buzzing about this Jesus of Nazareth who claimed to be the Messiah. He had been found guilty of blasphemy by the Sanhedrin, sentenced to death by the Roman governor, crucified, and buried in a secure tomb. But then the tomb was found to be empty and many witnesses claimed to have seen Jesus. They said He had been resurrected just as He had prophesied. Some had talked with Him and eaten with Him, and then had seen Him ascend into heaven.

Like all Jews, Saul had been waiting for the Messiah, but they were all looking for a warrior and conqueror; not a teacher, healer, and martyr. They believed Messiah would release them from the tyranny of Rome and make Israel the number one nation in the world again. Jesus of Nazareth hardly met their expectations by allowing the Romans to crucify Him. And He and His disciples were from Galilee, which was basically a hick town where the people were not very well educated.

We can imagine how Saul, being a great thinker, might come to Jerusalem and investigate all the stories and rumors he has heard about this Jesus. He probably went to the High Priest and asked, "What's going on? What do you know about Jesus of Nazareth?"

The priest said, "Saul, I tell you, I can't understand. Jesus came riding into Jerusalem on a donkey about a week before Passover and the whole city went crazy over Him. They even put their cloaks on the ground and waved palm leaves to worship Him! As He passed they cried, 'Son of David! Blessed is He who comes in the name of the Lord! Hosanna in the highest!'

"If it wasn't bad enough that He let people worship Him, then He claimed to be the Son of God! So we arrested Him and beat Him, but He wouldn't say a word. Then we took Him to Pilate, who whipped Him. The Romans really mangled His body, and then they crucified Him for all to see.

"We put a sixteen-man guard and a huge stone at the door of the tomb where His dead body was laid. Three days later the stone was rolled away, the guards were freaked out, and now the people are saying that Jesus was raised from the dead! It's so obvious that those Galileans stole His body." The High Priest was fuming with rage, and Saul had grown more and more angry as he listened. He decided to go out on the streets and hear what others had to say.

Saul was infuriated to find that many Jews believed that this Jesus really had been raised from the dead. He would stop them and say, "Wait a minute! The High Priest told me that you stole His body."

The answer was always the same, "No! We didn't steal His body. He was raised from the dead. He was the Lamb of God, who took away the sin of the world. His blood was shed for us. Now He is alive and reigns forevermore, just like the prophets foretold."

Saul returned to the High Priest in a rage. "What are you going to do about this?"

He said, "Well, I just don't know what I'm going to do."

And Saul said, "Then I'll do it! Just give me the authority to drag these 'believers' in and we'll teach them not to worship this blasphemer."

That's when Saul of Tarsus began to persecute the church. He arrested and persecuted anyone who named the name of Jesus. He threw them into jail and sometimes had them killed. We first hear of Saul in Acts, chapter 7. Stephen is being tried before the Sanhedrin and preaches the gospel to them, which infuriates all the religious Jews. So they decide to stone Stephen.

When they heard these things, they were cut to the heart, and they gnashed on him with their teeth.

But he, being full of the Holy Ghost, looked up stedfastly into heaven, and saw the glory of God, and Jesus standing on the right hand of God,

And said, Behold, I see the heavens opened, and the Son of man standing on the right hand of God.

Then they cried out with a loud voice, and stopped their ears, and ran upon him with one accord,

> *And cast him out of the city, and stoned him: and the witnesses*
> *laid down their clothes at a young man's feet, whose name was Saul.*
>
> ACTS 7:54-58

Nothing makes religious people more angry than when the Spirit of God shows up on a truly righteous believer like Stephen. He is telling them the truth that they do not want to hear and refuse to accept. He's knocking over every "sacred cow" they ever had. But what's interesting is that we know from verse 58 that Saul of Tarsus is hearing the whole message, whether he likes it or not. He is also part of the mob that stones Stephen, and that means he witnessed the following.

> *And they stoned Stephen, calling upon God, and saying, Lord*
> *Jesus, receive my spirit.*
>
> *And he kneeled down, and cried with a loud voice, Lord, lay not*
> *this sin to their charge. And when he had said this, he fell asleep.*
>
> ACTS 7:59,60

This only made Saul more angry and determined to wipe out every believer in Jesus of Nazareth.

> *And Saul was consenting unto his death. And at that time there*
> *was a great persecution against the church which was at Jerusalem;*
> *and they were all scattered abroad throughout the regions of Judaea*
> *and Samaria, except the apostles.*
>
> *And devout men carried Stephen to his burial, and made great*
> *lamentation over him.*
>
> *As for Saul, he made havock of the church, entering into every*
> *house, and haling men and women committed them to prison.*
>
> ACTS 8:1-3

You have to realize that Saul thought he was doing God a favor. He thought he was preserving the faith in the one true God. He was getting rid of heretics, who were saying Jesus was raised from the dead and was the Messiah. How could Messiah be a Galilean? Didn't they realize how foolish that was? God would never do that.

Saul persecuted and killed believers. That was his new job description as a Pharisee of the Pharisees. He became a hero to the religious Jews, but a terrible enemy to the believers in Jesus.

> *And Saul, yet breathing out threatenings and slaughter against the disciples of the Lord, went unto the high priest,*
>
> *And desired of him letters to Damascus to the synagogues, that if he found any of this way, whether they were men or women, he might bring them bound unto Jerusalem.*
>
> ACTS 9:1,2

At this time Saul had just obtained letters from the High Priest in Jerusalem, which gave him permission to go to the synagogue in Damascus and arrest any Jew who believed that Jesus was the Messiah, man or woman. But he never accomplished his mission.

> *And as he journeyed, he came near Damascus: and suddenly there shined round about him a light from heaven:*
>
> *And he fell to the earth, and heard a voice saying unto him, Saul, Saul, why persecutest thou me?*
>
> *And he said, Who art thou, Lord? And the Lord said, I am Jesus whom thou persecutest: it is hard for thee to kick against the pricks.*
>
> ACTS 9:3-5

In the middle of the day, a light shone from heaven that was brighter than the noonday sun. Saul knew there was only one light that was brighter than the sun, and that light was the Shekinah glory of God. And out of the light comes this voice which speaks and says, "Saul! Saul! Why do you persecute Me?"

"Lord, who are You?"

And this answer was the answer that changed his life forever. He said, "I am Jesus, whom you persecute."

Why didn't He say, "I'm the Messiah" or "I'm God Almighty"? But instead He says, "I'm Jesus." He tells Saul that He is Jesus because that conveyed only one meaning, that Jesus was the Son of God and the Messiah. And Saul is confronted with the worst thing a religious man can be confronted with: he is wrong.

We have to hand it to Saul, though, because he doesn't sit down and cry and feel sorry for himself. And he doesn't die of shame right there on the road. Instead, he asks Jesus what He wants him to do next.

> And he trembling and astonished said, Lord, what wilt thou have me to do? And the Lord said unto him, Arise, and go into the city, and it shall be told thee what thou must do.
>
> ACTS 9:6

Because he has been blinded by the glory of God, Saul is led by the hand to the house of Judas, a believer. He is there for three days, not eating or sleeping, just praying and waiting on God. We can imagine what was going on in his incredible brain at this point. Remember, Saul knows the Old Testament backwards and forwards. He knows all the messianic prophecies. *Jesus was crucified; now He's alive. If He is the sacrifice to end all sacrifices, then there's no more reason for sacrifices. If He's the Lamb of God who's taken away the sin of the world, then the law has been fulfilled.*

Then the Lord did something interesting. In Acts 9:10-16 He appeared in a vision to a man named Ananias, a regular believer who was just minding his own business. He said, "Ananias."

Ananias answered, "Yes, Lord!"

"Go over to Judas's house. A man named Saul of Tarsus is there praying, and he is waiting for you."

Ananias was a little worried at this and said, "But Lord, I've heard of this guy. He is really wicked, and he's hurt a lot of believers."

But the Lord said, "It's okay, Ananias. I know what he's done, but he's one of Mine. I'm going to use him to reach the Gentiles, and I'll show him the things he'll suffer for Me. So you go to him now."

> *And Ananias went his way, and entered into the house; and putting his hands on him said, Brother Saul, the Lord, even Jesus, that appeared unto thee in the way as thou camest, hath sent me, that thou mightest receive thy sight, and be filled with the Holy Ghost.*
>
> ACTS 9:17

Ananias stands before Saul and says two words that will change both men forever. He said, "Brother Saul." Saul of Tarsus was no longer the Lord's enemy or Ananias's enemy. He was his brother. Every bit of theology Saul had learned was completely altered. Everything that he had been taught from the time he was born was totally transformed by the revelation that Jesus of Nazareth was the Messiah. The Law had been fulfilled by a Person. No longer was life a matter of keeping the rules to please God the Judge. Instead, he would walk in the Spirit with the Father and the Son. Relationship instead of religion. Grace instead of legalism. Love instead of hate.

Saul had been accepted into the beloved (see Eph. 1:6). He was a child of God. And that was the most radical, revolutionary idea to ever hit his brain. Before he met Jesus on the road to Damascus, he didn't think God liked him unless he was doing something really important for Him. He believed God accepted him if he kept the law and made all the sacrifices to cleanse himself. But basically, God didn't like him. Now he grappled with the concept that God not only loved him, but He sent His Son Jesus to die on the cross for him.

Saul became Paul. A new life meant a new name.

Paul didn't have to worry about what God thought about him, how to please Him, or if he was accepted by Him. Worry was replaced by the Word, and fear was replaced by faith.

MY TESTIMONY

Unlike Saul of Tarsus, my beginnings were nothing to boast about unless you were an enemy of God. I grew up in the city of Chicago, Illinois, and have lived there my entire life. I went to a Catholic school some of the time and public school the rest of the time. My memory is that I was told at a young age that I was stupid, that I didn't have anything going for me, and nobody wanted to be around me. And what I remembered people said to me and the way they treated me determined the way I saw myself. I believed I was rejected and alone because I was a worthless, stupid person.

When I was in the eighth grade I began to drink, and by the time I was sixteen I was an alcoholic. Both my parents were alcoholics, and I lived in a world of hurt. As a result I went around hurting anybody I possibly could and called it fun. To screw up a person's life was a joy to me. That made my week, and I would have given a week, to mess up a person's life.

At sixteen I also worked at a store that carried a variety of things, but it also had a very large liquor cooler. A couple of us would build little forts in there and drink. The boss never could find us, and I was drunk on the job all the time. During the summer we were displaying lounge chairs, and I remember passing out in one of them while I was working, right in the middle of the store!

Then one day my boss said to me, "You know something? I know you're stealing from me."

I said, "Yeah, and you can't catch me either."

I knew that I had a problem. I didn't know what it was or where it was coming from, but it felt like pressure. Things weren't going the way I wanted them to go, and I was always upset. To compensate for all this pressure and anxiety, I drank and did all kinds of immoral things. Any bad thoughts were filed away where no one would know because I was afraid of what people would think about me.

I lived a life of thievery and drunkenness until I was about eighteen years old. Linda was seventeen, and we had started to spend time together. We had been going out for three months when something really wild happened to me. It was August 31, 1972, and I was driving my 1968 442 Oldsmobile. A gentleman walked up, pulled a gun on me, and told me to get out of my car. Being drunk and totally uncooperative, I sped away, ran traffic signals, and ended up crashing that particular car at 140 miles an hour. Miraculously, I walked away unhurt.

I know cars, and after the wreck I could not tell what kind of car it was. They told me that the steering wheel was stuck through my seat. So I wasn't sure how I got out of the car. Then my mother did something that was very out of character for her. The next day when I was wondering out loud just why I was still alive, she prophesied to me. She said, "God has something for you to do with your life."

In Chapter 7 I told you a little bit about my mother, who was an alcoholic, drug addict, and gypsy. At that time, if Bozo the Clown had come down our street, knocked on our door, and told my mother that he was God, she would have believed him! She did not know God. I don't blame either one of my parents for my upbringing because they didn't know better. I'm just glad God had mercy on us and extended His grace to us.

My father has passed away, but they both accepted Jesus as their personal Lord and Savior.

When my mother told me that God had something for me to do with my life, I just said, "Yeah lady, get out of my room."

For three more years I continued in confusion and emotional pain, being hurt and hurting others. I did have a revelation that liquor was evil, however, so I started doing drugs instead. Drugs actually made me worse, but you couldn't smell them on me. So now I thought I had it all together. I was high but I wasn't stinking or slobbering. I was cool.

Linda and I got married in 1974. I married her because I needed her. I needed her input in my life because I knew my life was nothing, I was going nowhere, and I didn't ever expect to go anywhere. She didn't need me, but I needed her. I didn't really love her, but it seemed like it might bring some kind of meaning to my life.

I was married when I was twenty-one, and by the time I was twenty-two I thought that I had gotten rid of all the bad stuff in my life, and I would never have to deal with it again. Of course, I hadn't dealt with it at all! I had just shoved it in a corner of my brain or drugged it away.

The pressure was still there. To me, it seemed that life wouldn't allow me to be a nice guy. I had to be mean to survive. Life made me to be the kind of person I didn't want to be. So I was continuously disappointed and disillusioned with myself. I didn't want to be the person I was, but there was nothing I could do about it because I had to protect myself. That meant putting up walls so that no one could see me. When someone hurt me, I decided no one would ever take advantage of me like that again. All those bricks of hurt turned into a wall of hate for God and for others, but mostly for myself. And I lived inside that wall, thinking that it was the only thing that would protect me from more hurt and pain.

When Linda and I had been married for about a year and four months I started working downtown. The company imported audio equipment from England and Japan, and I jumped out of the frying pan into the fire. I entered a world of sexual experience and other kinds of immoral behavior that are just too depraved to describe here. The people I was around had every type of sexual appetite imaginable and unimaginable, and they lived their lives for these experiences.

In the middle of all of that, I looked down the corridor of life and said to myself, "Now wait, if I have all of these vices at twenty-two years of age, and if all there is to life is to grow up, try to make a living, come home, get loaded, love somebody else's wife and not your own, have a wife, a couple of kids, a dog, a house with a white picket fence, get old, be put in a rest home, be rejected by your children, wear Depends, and then die—if that's all there is to life—then this is my philosophy: Live fast, die young, and be a good looking corpse."

And that's what I did. But it didn't kill the pain or even provide an acceptable way to survive through life. So very solemnly and very openly I tried to kill myself on a couple of occasions. One time I decided I would drive my car into a concrete embankment at about one hundred miles per hour. But for some reason one of my hands stopped me.

Then one day my mind snapped. The pressure had reached a level where, all of a sudden, every subconscious fear that I had stuffed deep in my brain became conscious. I went into massive panic, but I knew what to do. All I had to do was get loaded again. Then it would go away. *This is just a bad day,* I thought, *and tomorrow will be better.* The only problem was, that day turned into a week. And the week turned into a month. At night Linda would say to me, "I have got to sleep. Can you just get out of bed?" She said this because my heart was beating so hard she could hear it, and it was keeping her awake!

The only time I could sleep was when I ran and worked out so hard that I was absolutely exhausted, but sometimes even that didn't work. I was so tired, but when I laid down to try to rest every worry came back, and I would be seized with panic all over again. I would think, *Why did this happen to me? Why me? Why is this going on in my life?*

What I didn't realize was that everything I had ever worried about—things that had not happened to me and might not ever happen to me—were all coming at me at once. Worry, fear, and anxiety are usually based on something that is not real, that is not true, and that has no basis in reality. Worry is an anticipation over something that might or could happen but probably won't happen.

After three months of panic attacks, not eating or sleeping, being absolutely paranoid about everything, I was frazzled. Voices were talking to me. They would tell me, "Just one pull of the wheel and all of this will be over in a second!" They spoke things like that to me minute after minute, hour after hour, all day long, day after day. It was not unusual for me to have five to seven conversations going on in my head at one time. I was so preoccupied with them that I couldn't hear anything anyone else was saying.

I knew my life was a wreck, and I thought that the only place to find God was at church. There was a church downtown near my work, so I went in there one day. I thought Jesus was living there because there were life-size statues of all of His friends in the building. So I knelt down in the second row, and I said, "God, I'm wrecked. My life is in shambles. I need help, and I need it yesterday."

126

I felt no better. The voices were screaming so loud now that I got up and walked out. I was almost out the door when another voice spoke to me, a voice I had never heard before. It said, "Hold on, Son. Everything's going to be all right. Don't give up." Things on the outside were no better. Things on the inside were no better. But this voice brought peace. It brought rest and hope.

After this the voices bore down upon me more than ever, trying to get me to kill myself and do terrible things. But I resisted them. Don't let anybody tell you that if you're not a Christian you can't resist the devil. Any human being can resist the devil. All you need to do is tell him no.

I remember banging my fist on the table, yelling at the voices, "No, no, no, no! I won't believe that! I won't do that!" I had no idea why I was doing what I was doing. The truth is, I've probably *fallen* into more things right in my life than I ever consciously tried to do right! Nevertheless, Linda finally faced the fact that yelling at voices and banging on the table wasn't really normal behavior.

What I like about Linda is that she is a strong woman. She does not buckle under pressure. She refuses to give up and throw in the towel. This was a time when it seemed as though quitting was the best option, but she chose not to and stuck with me. Today, God has radically transformed our lives.

On October 4, 1975, at 11:00 A.M., I saw a psychiatrist. By 11:15 I was in a mental institution. No "passing Go." No picking up your clothes. No going home first. "You don't have to do anything. We'll make sure you're all right. We'll be there with you. This is where you're going."

All I said was, "Well, that's really nice." When I got to the mental hospital, I felt safe behind the locked door. Then the first thing they did was to drug me. I was used to that! I wanted to know if they had any more! I went from loaded to blitzed. I went on living at the level of handling life by drugging myself.

My time in the mental institution was highly educational. They did very funny things with me and the rest of the crazy people. But let me tell you something. Some people who are in mental institutions are not crazy; they are hurt. If you want a real conversation about the worst issues of life, go talk to somebody in a mental ward. You will get past all the niceties immediately. I know because I've been there.

I was diagnosed with what's called "ambiguous anxiety," which means that you have no idea which way to go from moment to moment. Later on they changed my diagnosis to a deep character disorder. I said, "Doc, what does that mean?"

He said, "All it means is, nothing can be done for you. The way you are is the way you'll be forever. I'll drug you to get you past the hump, but you'll be this way the rest of your life."

I said, "Well, isn't that a nice thing to say?"

He said, "Oh, I wouldn't let it bother you."

I'm thinking, *Wouldn't let it bother me?* I said, "Why is that?"

He said, "Because I feel the way you do sometimes."

Now I'm thinking, *You are sitting on the wrong side of the desk! Come over here, Doc. You can pay me. I'll get on your side of the desk. You feel like I do? I do not need to talk to you if you feel like I do. I need to talk to somebody who knows how to get out of this, not somebody who's in it.*

I said, "You know, I mean, that's my life."

The doctor said, "Well son, honestly, there's nothing that can be done for you."

After staying there four times longer than they wanted anyone to stay at that particular mental hospital, a certain fellow got a job there. About the second evening he was there,

I noticed there was something different about him. I couldn't make him mad by calling him every dirty word I knew. He was ruining the only sport I had with people that made any sense. You see, if I could make you mad, then that made me happy. I was still depressed, but now you were mad, which made me feel better than you.

One night this guy asked me where I would go if I died. I said, "I'll go to heaven."

He said, "Why is that?"

I said, "'Cause I'm a nice guy. I don't hurt anybody, and I don't wanna hurt me. That's one of the reasons why I'm here. I'm a nice person. I keep the commandments." (I was glad he didn't ask me what they were!)

Then he shocked me. He said, "That's not good enough."

I said, "What do you mean that's not good enough?"

He said, "If you could get to heaven by being good, why did Jesus Christ die for the sins of the world?"

I said, "I never thought of that. Why don't you tell me just a little bit more?"

In the next few hours something extraordinary happened. It was getting very late, and if you were up too late the men in the white coats would put straitjackets on you. So you did not stay up too late! You were in bed at 11:30 P.M. But now it's midnight, and nobody's saying anything to us. That was the first miracle. The second miracle was that in places like this, employees are not allowed to tell patients about Jesus. But this guy was telling me everything he ever heard about Him—and he told me how God loved me.

I said, "Wait a minute! You gotta be good. You gotta be a good person. And you gotta go to church on Sundays. And you gotta go to confession. You gotta keep the sacraments. You can't go to heaven without the sacraments."

Hour after hour, time and time again, he told me about God's love for me. Finally, I came face to face with an insurmountable love. The One I thought was always mad at me was the One who loved me. I had blamed the wrong person! I blamed Him my whole life. I had judged Him for the way my life was. I had shaken my fist at Him and said, "You're too hard. You're too tough," to the point where I had said, "That's it! I'm finished with You! I can't try to be good. The more I try, the worse it gets, so I give up. I'm fed up with You."

Now, like Saul of Tarsus on the road to Damascus, I was faced with an entirely different reality than I had lived all my life. In the middle of the night on October 28, 1975, I said, "God, if You're real, I want to know You; and if You're not, get the hell out of my life! I don't even want to hear about You, about this love, if I can't have this love. If I can't experience You, I don't want You. I don't want You around me. I don't want to hear Your name. I don't want to hear anything about You anymore if I can't know You."

I spewed out every horrible thing I felt. If what this man was saying was true, then everything I had ever believed about God was a lie. I had thought He was up there in heaven holding a big hammer, just waiting for me to mess up so He could pound me. This love thing was not at all what I had believed.

Then the man said, "God loves you. He'll answer your prayers."

I said, "Without worrying?"

"Without worrying. As a matter of fact, you look like a freak when you worry. You look funny to God when you worry. Because it's like telling the whole wide universe you don't really believe God's telling you the truth."

Then I got down on my knees, bowed my head, and said, "Jesus, I can't make it. I'm bankrupt. Here I am. Come into my life. I have nothing to offer You. I'm not good at anything. I'm not even good at losing. Matter of fact, I'm just not good. After years of alcoholism, drug abuse, sexual abuse, stealing, lying, and everything that I can think of, I sicken myself, and I don't want to live. Jesus, if You can do anything with my life, I'm giving it to You, and I want to know You. I don't want to play a game. I don't want to be religious. I just want to know You. I don't want to go to church unless You're there. Whatever You want to do with me, do it, but I don't want to know You for a week and then be put on a shelf. I want all the marbles. I don't want no junk. I want what's real."

Then the fellow gave me his Bible, and I went to bed holding it. I didn't know if you were supposed to hold the Bible, but it felt good to hold it. When I was growing up, when you saw a Bible you were afraid to touch it. It belonged to God, you know, and we were all scared of God. Why? Because we thought He was mad at us. My whole life I had thought He was mad at me.

On October 29, at 8:00 in the morning, I woke up a brand-new man. My life was 180 degrees different. Some people ask me why they didn't see a lot of real dramatic changes in their lives right after they got saved the way I did. I just tell them, "Well honey, you weren't demon possessed like I was!"

My whole perception of God had changed.

My whole perception of myself had changed.

My whole perception of the world had changed.

One day I was a raving lunatic, and the next day I was completely delivered. When I had gone to bed the night before, I had tried to get one of the nurses to go with me. When I woke up the next morning, I was repenting for what I had done. Jesus touched me while I was sleeping. He had had me on the Holy Ghost operating table, and He changed my life. I was free!

Walking down the hallway the next morning, I saw the woman who pushed a little cart that contained things like hair scissors, rollers, bobby pins, and that kind of stuff. They wouldn't let us have any of those things for fear we would hurt ourselves or each other, but she would use them to do things for us. That morning I asked her to cut my beard close enough so that I could shave it. They let us have a razor, but it was the kind you couldn't hurt yourself with.

So she cut my beard and then I said, "Please, give me a haircut."

The man who used to live inside Robb Thompson died on October 28, 1975, when I received Jesus Christ as my Lord and Savior. That old man was riddled with worry, fear, and anxiety. But the new man came out of that mental ward *thoroughly* saved and delivered.

For about six months after I was released Linda and I lived with her mother. This was a trying time. I was a changed man, but not everything about me changed. I was new on the inside, but I still had some work to do on the outside. Living with Linda's family was difficult, and I had to build trust with them. But it didn't take long for them to see the change in my life. They saw how Jesus had changed my life and was continuing to change my life. When I learned that the Bible says, "Let him who steals steal no more," I got a job to work with my hands, stacking pallets. I wasn't going to steal like I used to. Then I got a job for a parcel delivery service. I began to tell people about Jesus and pray with them whenever I could.

BURYING THE PAST WITH JESUS

People ask me, "Why are you so dedicated to the Word?"

I answer, "I don't have anything else."

Maybe some Christians are lukewarm because their lives weren't quite bad enough when Jesus saved them. There was nothing in my past that I wanted to hold on to unless Jesus told me to hold on to it. There was no future in my past. He had given me the gift of a clean slate, a fresh start, a new life, and a future with hope.

For the first time in my life, I wasn't worrying about all the horrible things I had done and how mad God must be at me. I wasn't worried about the mistakes I was going to make in the future because my life was so messed up. In fact, as a new creature in Christ Jesus, I wasn't worrying at all—and that was a miracle!

Like the apostle Paul, I was consumed and overwhelmed with God's mercy and grace. Here he gives his testimony.

> *Though I might also have confidence in the flesh. If any other man thinketh that he hath whereof he might trust in the flesh, I more:*
>
> *Circumcised the eighth day, of the stock of Israel, of the tribe of Benjamin, an Hebrew of the Hebrews; as touching the law, a Pharisee;*
>
> *Concerning zeal, persecuting the church; touching the righteousness which is in the law, blameless.*
>
> *But what things were gain to me, those I counted loss for Christ.*
>
> PHILIPPIANS 3:4-7

Paul had everything going for him as a religious Pharisee. I had nothing going for me as a nonreligious drunk, drug addict, and morally depraved person. Yet Jesus died for both of us, saved both of us, and both of us were never the same. From the time we were saved, nothing mattered but Jesus.

> *Yea doubtless, and I count all things but loss for the excellency of the knowledge of Christ Jesus my Lord: for whom I have suffered the loss of all things, and do count them but dung, that I may win Christ,*
>
> *And be found in him, not having mine own righteousness, which is of the law, but that which is through the faith of Christ, the righteousness which is of God by faith:*

That I may know him, and the power of his resurrection, and the
fellowship of his sufferings, being made conformable unto his death.

PHILIPPIANS 3:4-10

The worries, fears, anxieties, and panic attacks of the past
were left at the cross. We were no longer righteous because we
kept the law or did good deeds but because Jesus shed His
blood on the cross to cleanse us from all unrighteousness and
make us holy and acceptable to God. Do you remember when
Saul met Jesus on the road to Damascus? Jesus asked him why
he was persecuting Him because He wanted Saul to understand
that He identified with His Church. But after Saul was saved
and became Paul, Jesus never mentioned it again!

God isn't bringing up what you did in the past. In His Word
He tells you to forget it, walk away from it, and walk with Him
in a new life. You'll never make your past right, so there is no
reason to worry about it. He took care of it at the cross. Now
your job is to move forward with Him in the life He has for you.

Not as though I had already attained, either were already
perfect: but I follow after, if that I may apprehend that for which also
I am apprehended of Christ Jesus.

Brethren, I count not myself to have apprehended: but this one
thing I do, forgetting those things which are behind, and reaching
forth unto those things which are before,

I press toward the mark for the prize of the high calling of God
in Christ Jesus.

PHILIPPIANS 3:12-14

My past only goes back as far as that which is written. I can't
go back one moment before the moment I was saved because my
past ended there. Through Jesus Christ, I was set free from all
worry about my past and was free to go forward with joy and
peace instead of fear and anxiety. What a miracle, praise God!

Keeping Priorities Straight

When I got saved, I thought I wouldn't have to deal with worrying and fear and torment any longer. Then one day during the Christmas rush, while I was working for the parcel delivery service, an incident occurred that changed everything. They had filled up my truck with so many packages that when I tried to open the inside door to deliver the first package, it wouldn't open. The boxes were jammed against it.

I yanked and yanked and pulled and pulled, but the door wouldn't budge. So I decided to go around to the back of the truck and open the back door. I would just have to take all the packages out and rearrange them on the sidewalk. But evidently they shoved every box they could inside and then shoved in ten more. When they slammed the door shut, the latch was embedded in the back of a huge box, and it wouldn't come out. When I tried to pull the latch, it wouldn't open.

All of a sudden, without thinking, I ran around to the front of the truck, got into the driver's seat, and began to drive. I drove and drove and drove until I finally asked myself the question, "Where are you going?" At that moment terror struck me. Anxiety like I hadn't known for years came back to me.

Since I had become a Christian, I had confessed the Word more than any other believer I knew. I had stood on the Word more than anyone else I knew. I got up that morning having everything going for me, but now I had everything on top of me! What was happening? How was I going to fix this?

Next I was terrified that I really didn't believe what I said I believed. I wondered if I had gone through the motions of confessing the Word of God like daily calisthenics. Had I ever checked to see if what I believed was really down on the inside of me? The panic and terror became a double nightmare. On top of being freaked out, I was having a crisis of faith.

In this state you feel like you're dying and your life is completely out of control. It's not a bad day or a poor mental outlook. It's not just temporary depression that you can't seem to shake. You are completely gripped by terror and can experience a multitude of symptoms: dry mouth, heart palpitations, irregular or increased heartbeat, nausea, diarrhea, chills, hot flashes, trembling, and even violent shaking. You think you're having a heart attack or dying of some dread disease.

As believers, we have to understand that there is a reason this happens: we have gotten our priorities all messed up. Probably for longer than we would care to admit, we have been focusing on things we shouldn't have been focusing on. We think we're living a good, Christian life, but we have slowly wandered off the path.

KINGDOM FIRST

When we are saved, we are saved to worship God. He gives us things not so that things will own us, but so those things will enable us to declare His glory to a world that doesn't know Him. He gives us peace not so we can live the life we want to live, but so that we can live the life He's called us to live.

> *Therefore take no thought, saying, What shall we eat? or, What shall we drink? or, Wherewithal shall we be clothed?*

(For after all these things do the Gentiles seek:) for your heavenly Father knoweth that ye have need of all these things.

But seek ye first the kingdom of God, and his righteousness; and all these things shall be added unto you.

MATTHEW 6:31-33

What is a Christian's first priority? Seeking the kingdom of God and His righteousness. Sad to say, there are many Christians whose first priority is a combination of material things and their own pleasure. Many people have gotten saved because they believe God's going to make them rich and they'll finally get all the things they want. They use their relationship with God for gain. The apostle Paul dealt with that in 1 Timothy 6:5 when he said that many think that godliness is gain. He also said, "From such withdraw yourself." We are not to fellowship with those kinds of believers.

Then there are believers in the other extreme who believe if godliness is not gain then godliness must be poverty. They believe God wants His people to be poor so they will be holy. But Jesus set the record straight when He said, "Don't think about your food. Don't think about your drink. Don't think about your clothes. Don't think about your house. Don't think about your car. Don't think about your bank account. Don't spend your time worrying about money and material things. Think about the kingdom of God."

Are you supposed to be a good steward of everything you own? Yes, but those things should never be a priority. I can't tell you how many times I've seen believers neglect or even forget about their relationship with God because He gives them such a great business. They become so busy with the business that they quit worshiping and serving Him.

Let me help you with how this works. You get saved, life is so much better, you start being successful in areas you always struggled in before, and then you forget to read your Bible and pray for a couple of days. A couple of weeks after that you skip Sunday service. Then you realize you haven't read your Bible or prayed in about a month, but you're too busy to deal with it right now. Soon you are completely out of fellowship with God, and you haven't got a clue—but you think you have a clue! You keep lying to yourself that you can live your life the way you want and be okay. After all, you're doing good things and being a good person. It's not like you're robbing banks and shooting people.

One day it's all going to come falling down on you, and you'll be back on your face before God, trying to salvage your messed-up existence by begging Him for help. So you start back into the routine of praying and reading your Bible every day. You get back into church and join the choir. And you're a little more determined to seek Him before your job, your hobbies, sports, or whatever else can take you away from putting Him first.

It's interesting that Jesus said that when you seek His kingdom first, "all these things shall be added unto you." He didn't say, "You'll have everything you want in a few days." So you don't need to get in a hurry. You don't need to try and multiply it. And you don't need to worry about whether it's going to come or not. It's going to come! Don't worry about it!

> *Take therefore no thought for the morrow: for the morrow shall take thought for the things of itself. Sufficient unto the day is the evil thereof.*
>
> MATTHEW 6:34

You don't ever need to worry about tomorrow because it may never come. You don't ever need to think about yesterday because there isn't anything that you can do about it. Yesterday is in the tomb; tomorrow's in the womb. All you have is now, the present time, because God lives in your now. And right now is where evil can come in and get you off-track. So what are you thinking about, seeking, and desiring right now? Is it a new car? Is it peace of mind? Or is it the kingdom of God and His righteousness?

What is your priority right now? Not tomorrow. Not next week. Not when you feel better or look better or have more money. If you are not seeking the kingdom of God first, then stop right now, repent, and get back on track with the Lord.

A REAL CONNECTION

Jesus dealt with the Pharisees in the same way I am challenging you right now.

> Woe unto you, scribes and Pharisees, hypocrites! for ye pay tithe of mint and anise and cummin, and have omitted the weightier matters of the law, judgment, mercy, and faith: these ought ye to have done, and not to leave the other undone.
>
> MATTHEW 23:23

As believers, we can't get into a rut and think we're okay because we do everything we're supposed to be doing either. Our relationship with Jesus has to be alive and in the now. We can't just read His Word and not meditate it and think about it. We can't pray a prayer we've practically memorized without really considering what we're saying and why we're saying it. We have to make sure that our hearts are with Him, that our focus is totally on Him. We have to be listening to His voice more than any other.

> If ye then be risen with Christ, seek those things which are above, where Christ sitteth on the right hand of God.
>
> Set your affection on things above, not on things on the earth.
>
> COLOSSIANS 3:1,2

I'm seeking what's in heaven, and what's in heaven? Jesus. I'm looking to see what He's doing and trying to hear what He's saying. And my affection isn't on what I'm going to have for dinner, what suit I'm wearing, what kind of car I'm driving, or how much money I have in my bank account. My affection is on God and everything that concerns Him.

> *For ye are dead, and your life is hid with Christ in God.*
> COLOSSIANS 3:3

Don't spend your time worrying about what's going on down here on earth because you are dead! You've already died. You died the moment you received Jesus as your Lord and Savior. You don't need to sit around and think about the things that are happening on earth because you are dead and your life is with Christ in God.

You must understand how important it is for you to make the things that are above a priority and to set your affections on the things of God. Otherwise, you will lose your taste for the things of God and not even recognize it. You'll be reading your Bible now and then and going to church on a fairly regular basis, but you won't be connecting with God. You'll just be giving Him a nod and going on your way. Pretty soon only the things of this world will excite you. You'll think you know everything—and then one day wake up and wonder how your life got to be such a mess.

In Isaiah 26:3 the Bible tells us that we'll have perfect peace if we keep our mind and heart on Jesus and trust Him in all things. "Perfect peace" is an interesting phrase because it is like peace on steroids. You will have such peace that nothing can worry you ever again—that is, if your mind is on God and you trust Him. If your mind is on God and not on yourself, your family, your friends, and everything else that concerns you, then all those things are going to be taken care of.

EATING HUMBLE PIE

I want to show you what happens to a man who fixes his priorities. Job was a man who lost his focus, then lost everything—including his health—and then fixed his priorities. Many believers feel like their life is like Job's, but they don't realize that somewhere along the way they lost their focus on the kingdom and put other things first. They let the Word of God become of no effect in their lives and quit acting on what they believed.

When you take for granted what you believe, and then things start going wrong, you begin to get offended with God. You start complaining, "How can I be living like this when I am a Christian? Why do I have to go through all of these things? Is this the way God treats His kids? I prayed and it didn't work for me."

Job got to the same place and God had to humble him for a few chapters. Here is part of what He said to Job.

> Then the LORD said to Job,
>
> "Do you still want to argue with the Almighty? You are God's critic, but do you have the answers?"
>
> Then the LORD answered Job from the whirlwind:
>
> "Brace yourself, because I have some questions for you, and you must answer them.
>
> Are you going to discredit my justice and condemn me so you can say you are right?
>
> Are you as strong as God, and can you thunder with a voice like his?
>
> All right then, put on your robes of state, your majesty and splendor.
>
> Give vent to your anger. Let it overflow against the proud.

Humiliate the proud with a glance; walk on the wicked where they stand.

Bury them in the dust. Imprison them in the world of the dead.

Then even I would praise you, for your own strength would save you.

JOB 42:1,2,6-14 NLT

God asks Job, "Are you really going to question my way of doing things? Do you really think you're as smart as I am? If that's the case, then I'd like to see your strength, wisdom, and ability to run the universe." In the *King James Version,* verse 14 reads, "Then will I also confess unto thee that thine own right hand can save thee." So God ends by saying, "If you can do all this, then I would have to say you can save yourself. You don't need Me."

Of course, Job knows there is no way he can save himself. He answers the Lord in great humility.

Then Job answered the LORD, and said,

I know that thou canst do every thing, and that no thought can be withholden from thee.

Who is he that hideth counsel without knowledge? therefore have I uttered that I understood not; things too wonderful for me, which I knew not.

JOB 42:1-3

Job says to God, "I recognize I have been thinking on my own. I've isolated myself or have gone to my friends for counsel. The last person I think about talking to is You. As a result I've uttered things that I don't really understand. I shot my mouth off and didn't even know what I was talking about."

I have heard of thee by the hearing of the ear: but now mine eye seeth thee.

Wherefore I abhor myself, and repent in dust and ashes.

JOB 42:5,6

At this point Job has realized how far he got from God. He was relying on his own thinking and judgment, then he turned to his friends. In the end he decided he was smarter than God. This is what happens when someone gets their priorities confused. They begin to trust in themselves, their friends, and the world around them. They ultimately blame God for all their troubles because they have gotten so far from His presence and His Word.

Seeking first God's kingdom and righteousness means seeking God first on every issue of your life. That is true humility.

Job saw that how low he had sunk was equal to how far he had moved away from seeking God's counsel and fellowship first. So he repented and simply moved back to the presence and Word of God, knowing that He was his only salvation. Job realized that he could not save himself. His friends couldn't save him. Nothing in the world could save him. Only God could save him.

When you realize that only God can save you—every second, every minute, every hour of every day—then your priorities are right. Because you are totally plugged into God above everything else, He can bless you and keep you.

THE SECOND PRIORITY

There's something more to be found in the book of Job about priorities, however. God is your first priority, but other people are your second priority, and God takes this very seriously. Jesus put it this way,

> And thou shalt love the Lord thy God with all thy heart, and with all thy soul, and with all thy mind, and with all thy strength: this is the first commandment.

And the second is like, namely this, Thou shalt love thy neighbour as thyself. There is none other commandment greater than these.

MARK 12:30,31

In the beginning of the book of Job, he was alone. He was so caught up in his worries about his children and all his wealth that he not only cut out that true connection with God, but he also didn't have time for his friends. He quit caring about others because he was so worried about all the things in his own life.

The devil wants to get you off by yourself every day so he can start talking to you. He wants to get you isolated from other believers and friends in the Lord because it's easier to introduce some real crazy thinking when someone is separated from their brothers and sisters in the Lord. That's how Satan did it to Eve, and that's how he does it to you.

It's so important for us to love God with all our hearts and then love our neighbors as ourselves. Not only is that a godly priority, but it also keeps us straight! Isn't it funny that when you say to your friends what you've been thinking in your mind, and they look at you like you just stepped off another planet, their look can jerk your mind back to the Word of God? All of a sudden you have godly perspective. You were carried away in your own thinking for a moment, but using other believers as a sounding board brought you back to the reality of God's truth.

In the end, that's how Job's situation completely turned around. First, he repented and got right with God. But things actually came back into place when he prayed for his friends. Job 42:10 says, "And the LORD turned the captivity of Job, when he prayed for his friends: also the LORD gave Job twice as much as he had before."

Because Job got his priorities in order, putting God first and then other people, he was blessed beyond his imagination. And the Bible tells us that he was never isolated and alone again.

> *Then came there unto him all his brethren, and all his sisters, and all they that had been of his acquaintance before, and did eat bread with him in his house: and they bemoaned him, and comforted him over all the evil that the LORD had brought upon him: every man also gave him a piece of money, and every one an earring of gold.*
>
> JOB 42:11

I want you to notice that after Job gets his priorities straight, all his friends and relatives start hanging out with him. He's not worried and terrified of what might happen to him anymore because he's completely trusting God and he cares for other people more than himself in a good way. This is when prosperity comes back into his life. People give him money and gold.

> *So the LORD blessed the latter end of Job more than his beginning: for he had fourteen thousand sheep, and six thousand camels, and a thousand yoke of oxen, and a thousand she asses.*
>
> *He had also seven sons and three daughters.*
>
> *And he called the name of the first, Jemima; and the name of the second, Kezia; and the name of the third, Kerenhappuch.*
>
> *And in all the land were no women found so fair as the daughters of Job: and their father gave them inheritance among their brethren.*
>
> *After this lived Job an hundred and forty years, and saw his sons, and his sons' sons, even four generations.*
>
> *So Job died, being old and full of days .*
>
> JOB 42:12-17

The Lord blessed Job with livestock. Somehow he and his wife manage to have more children (maybe the Lord changed her too)! And Job lives a long and happy life.

Once you stop seeking first God's kingdom and righteousness, it isn't long before worry, fear, and terror begin taking over your life. Worry wants you to stay at home. It makes you feel like that's the only place you're safe. Worry isolates you from the family of God and keeps you caged in torment. But when you get your priorities right and put God first in your life, you also have fellowship with other believers.

> And let us consider one another to provoke unto love and to good works:
>
> Not forsaking the assembling of ourselves together, as the manner of some is; but exhorting one another: and so much the more, as ye see the day approaching
>
> HEBREWS 10:24,25

This can happen the other way around, too. When you stop fellowshipping with other believers, it's easy to forget about God. It's also easy to listen more to the world and the devil than to the Word and the Spirit. We need each other in the body of Christ. We need other believers to provoke us to love and good works, to exhort each other to fight the good fight of faith.

Where are you right now? Are you at the place in your life where worry, fear, and terror have isolated you? Now is not the time to think you know it all. Some people think it's faith to say they don't need help, but it's really arrogance and stupidity. We all need help! Arrogance is the worst thing you'll ever face in your life because it will not allow you to confess your need for God and His people to help you through life. That's what Job realized, and that's what we all have to realize in order to get rid of worry and stay rid of worry.

True faith is founded on the humble understanding that you can't make it without God and His people. When you live your life according to this truth, staying intimately connected to God and the family of God, you will defeat worry every time it raises its ugly head in your life.

1 3

Coming to the Place of Peace

With so much turmoil going on in the world and many of our loved ones fighting in the Middle East, there is a tremendous amount of apprehension and fear among people. It is said that the entire world, more than ever before, is in the midst of fear. People don't know what's going to happen. When planes hit the World Trade Center Towers and the Pentagon, and a plane headed for the White House was brought down in Pennsylvania by its courageous passengers, life in America changed drastically.

President George W. Bush declared war on terror, but this war is different from any war we have ever fought. The rules are different. When the British came over to keep the United States from becoming an independent nation, they attacked as military forces had always attacked: in uniformed companies. Their companies of soldiers would stand against our companies of soldiers. Battalion after battalion marched toward one another and shot each other, and soldiers fell by the hundreds. But everyone could clearly recognize who their comrades were and who their enemies were.

During the beginning of the Revolutionary War, this was how fighting was done. But then the American troops learned how to go around the British and attack them from behind. And plain-clothes soldiers began to emerge, which made it harder for the British to recognize them as enemy soldiers and not civilians. Americans began to fight more along the lines of gorilla warfare.

In the War on Terror, the rules of war have changed once again. Our enemy could be anywhere at anytime, standing next to us at the bank, in the grocery store, or at a football game—strapped with explosives and ready to blow to bits himself or herself and everyone and everything around them. We're facing war within our gates.

KNOW THE PRINCE OF PEACE

How do we face these issues? How do we come to a place of peace in our lives? Let me tell you what happened to me a number of years ago. When I went into the mental institution in 1975, they expected me to be crazy forever. They told me that every year, from about Thanksgiving to Christmas, I would be checked into a mental hospital. That's the time of the year when it would fill up with people like me.

I lived with a tremendous amount of anxiety. My adrenaline flowed at an alarming rate, and my mind was running wild with fearful thoughts. I was continually being given drugs to calm me down, but God sent a man to tell me that Jesus would take care of me. He told me that Jesus would change my life because Jesus offered peace. He said Jesus' name is the Prince of Peace.

I said, "Well, I grew up in a denomination that never told me about this Prince of Peace that you're talking about." When I heard this, I thought "Prince of Peace" meant Jesus had a little crown on His head, and that was all that it meant. I said again, "I never heard that Jesus had this peace that you talk about."

Just for a moment I want to tell you what I was focusing on at that time in my life. I was focusing on what was happening to me on the outside, the situations and the circumstances that were going on in my life. These things actually were proving to me that I was a man filled with fear, filled with apprehension. I was someone who had my finger stuck in the proverbial light socket of life, and I lived that way for years. They told me I would live that way forever.

I was paranoid. I was afraid. I was apprehensive. I was ashamed. I was always suspicious. I believed I would never be free. And so I took every drug I could to try not to think about what was going on. I was focusing on the fact that I was afraid. What was I afraid of? I was afraid of *everything that was going on around me.*

In Luke 14:26 Jesus said, "Men's hearts will fail them for fear of things to come upon the earth." That was how I lived. I believed one day my heart would actually fail me because of the fear of things to come. It wasn't even things that were happening. It wasn't even things that were real. It was the fear of things that were coming.

Today people's hearts are failing them because of what is happening in the earth. The War on Terror is constantly on the media, and the secular media is so negative that they give absolutely no hope for anything. If you listen to them your life ends up being a paranoid wreck. Even a Christian can start freaking out because of all of the things that are coming upon the earth.

When I was in the mental institution, I discovered that I was listening more to what was happening around me and what might happen to me than who I was and what was happening on the inside of me. I was listening to reports that the economies around the world were in terrible shape, anti-American sentiment was throughout the world, and crime was so bad that anyone could creep up behind me and kill me if I walked down the street.

If I were still thinking like that, this is how it would go in my mind today. I would be thinking, *After church, when I go to my car, there's probably going to be somebody there who will jump me just because I'm an American, and worse, I'm a Christian preacher.* That would really be funny if it wasn't the truth! But it is the truth. American Christian preachers are key targets to the enemy we're facing today. And if I focused on that all the time, I would become so afraid that I probably would never leave my house. I certainly would not preach the gospel.

Obviously, this is not coming to a place of peace! There is only one way to come to the place of peace, and that way is the Prince of Peace. Jesus is the way, the truth, and the life; but He is also the Prince of Peace. I like that bumper sticker that says, "No Jesus, No Peace; Know Jesus, Know Peace." Jesus is the way you come to the place of peace.

TAKE THE BIBLE INTERNALLY

In Proverbs 29:18, Solomon tells us, "Without vision the people will run wild." The Bible lets us know that we must have the right vision or we're going to go crazy. Let me ask you a question. What are you focusing on? What do you think about all day? What is the thing that has either put the smile on your face and joy in your heart or is bothering you so much that everyone around you can tell you're scared to death?

To find the place of peace and overcome the worries in your life, one of the things you have to realize is that everything in your life will work according to what you believe on the inside. That's the reason we'll tell people to meditate on the Word of God when they come up in a prayer line. We will pray for them to be set free of all worry and anxiety, but the peace they get won't last very long if they go back to focusing on their worries instead of meditating in God's Word.

Then there are the ones who say, "I said that verse of Scripture 323 times and nothing ever changed!" I believe that is because they applied the Word topically instead of internally. God's Word has to be applied internally, deep in your heart. Jesus had a lot to say about this. We call this the parable of the sower. First, He told the parable.

> Once again Jesus began teaching by the lakeshore. There was such a large crowd along the shore that he got into a boat and sat down and spoke from there.
>
> He began to teach the people by telling many stories such as this one:
>
> "Listen! A farmer went out to plant some seed
>
> As he scattered it across his field, some seed fell on a footpath, and the birds came and ate it.
>
> Other seed fell on shallow soil with underlying rock. The plant sprang up quickly,
>
> but it soon wilted beneath the hot sun and died because the roots had no nourishment in the shallow soil.
>
> Other seed fell among thorns that shot up and choked out the tender blades so that it produced no grain.
>
> Still other seed fell on fertile soil and produced a crop that was thirty, sixty, and even a hundred times as much as had been planted."
>
> Then he said,
>
> "Anyone who is willing to hear should listen and understand!"
>
> MARK 4:1-9 NLT

This is a great story, but unfortunately none of the disciples understood what Jesus was talking about. They asked Him what He meant, and this is what He said to them.

> "But if you can't understand this story, how will you understand all the others I am going to tell?
>
> MARK 4:13 NLT

Did you get what Jesus just said? He said that if we don't understand the parable of the sower, we're not going to understand any of the other parables. And since Jesus taught mostly in parables, that means we're not going to understand most of what He taught. He didn't leave us wondering and frustrated, however. He told us exactly what the parable of the sower means.

> *The farmer I talked about is the one who brings God's message to others.*
>
> *The seed that fell on the hard path represents those who hear the message, but then Satan comes at once and takes it away from them.*
>
> *The rocky soil represents those who hear the message and receive it with joy.*
>
> *But like young plants in such soil, their roots don't go very deep. At first they get along fine, but they wilt as soon as they have problems or are persecuted because they believe the word.*
>
> *The thorny ground represents those who hear and accept the Good News,*
>
> *but all too quickly the message is crowded out by the cares of this life, the lure of wealth, and the desire for nice things, so no crop is produced.*
>
> *But the good soil represents those who hear and accept God's message and produce a huge harvest—thirty, sixty, or even a hundred times as much as had been planted."*
>
> MARK 4:14-20 NLT

Let's read this in the *King James Version* because the language is closer to understanding that the power of God is found in receiving His Word deep into our hearts. It isn't just a message; it is the living Word of God received into the good ground of our hearts that brings forth fruit in our lives.

> *The sower soweth the word.*
>
> *And these are they by the way side, where the word is sown; but when they have heard, Satan cometh immediately, and taketh away the word that was sown in their hearts.*

In Joshua, God had already given the Promised Land to the children of Israel. But He had to tell Joshua to have courage and to stay in His Word day and night to remember what God had already said and to come to the place where he believed what God said, the place of peace. If Joshua couldn't believe that God's Word was true and stand on it in peace, God knew he wouldn't be able to do what God needed him to do to take the Promised Land.

When God came to Jeremiah and said, "I've called you to be a prophet unto the nations," Jeremiah said that he was a baby. God said, "Don't say you're a baby because I didn't say you are a baby. I said you are My prophet." Jeremiah decided to believe what God said about him instead of what he thought about himself or what other people might think about him. As a result, he came to the place of peace and was able to be the prophet God needed him to be.

The angel called Gideon a mighty man of valor and Gideon said, "Wait a minute! I'm the runt of my family, which is the runt of the tribe, which is the runt of the clan. Do you understand? I'm no mighty man of valor!" But God didn't back down. Finally Gideon accepted he was who God said he was, coming to the place of peace, and then he could do what God called him to do.

To get free and stay free of worry, fear, anxiety, apprehension, and all that kind of bondage we need to do exactly what God told Joshua to do: meditate the Word of God day and night. And then we need to make the decision that will change everything in our lives: we will believe what God says and not what we think or others think. Deciding that God's Word is true above all other things makes our hearts good ground. And we have already seen from Mark, chapter 4, that when the Word goes into good ground it brings forth fruit thirty-, sixty-, and one hundred-fold.

The fruit I'm talking about is the fruit of the Spirit. Love, joy, and peace are the first three mentioned in Galatians 5:22, and nowhere in the list do you find worry! The peace that passes all understanding that comes from the Prince of Peace is ours when we make the decision to believe what God says about us and our lives.

TALK TO YOURSELF

When I got saved I really got saved. I can tell you where I was, what I was doing, and every detail. My life was completely changed because of the blood of Jesus, and no one can ever talk me out of it. But I thought that being saved meant I would never have another bad thought. Maybe you believed that as well. And when Mr. Ugly started introducing his ugly thoughts to my brain, I thought I was a terrible person.

Mr. Ugly would say, "You don't like that guy. He's stupid." I realized I didn't like him and went home filled with anger, resentment, and guilt. Then I begged God to forgive me. "Oh, God, please forgive me. I never wanted to hate anybody. I guess I hate someone now." And then I'd get all these other wicked thoughts. Instead of feeling like a Christian, I felt like a demon with skin on it!

This happens to every new believer. We get saved and think everything's going to be perfect because Jesus made us to be perfect. He'll see to it that we'll never have another conflict in our lives. Not! The enemy begins to introduce all kinds of evil thoughts and we think we're not good—in fact, we can't think anything good. We become a wreck. We're rededicating our lives to Jesus at every altar call. And it seems that we spend most of our time asking for forgiveness and begging God to change us.

We need to understand that failure is imminent if we spend more time *listening* to ourselves than *talking* to ourselves.

Everything in life that God ever created has ears, and He's called us to talk to it. What we are supposed to say to whatever we're talking to, especially ourselves? We are to say exactly what God's Word says.

When you do this things will begin to change inside you. Peace will replace worry. You're no longer topically applying the Scriptures; you are taking them internally, letting them go deep into your soul and spirit. You're meditating God's Word day and night, choosing to believe what God says; and if Mr. Ugly tries to lie to you, you speak God's truth right back to him. That's coming to the place of peace.

The Perfect Place

Some people change their environments. They decide their environment is bad and if their environment is good then they'll be good. Staying away from the bars and people who drink will definitely help an alcoholic to keep from drinking, but until the alcoholic deals with the root of the problem inside, they will always be craving a drink. They will continue to be enslaved to the enemy of their souls.

The same is true with worry. You can move to the perfect place and continue to worry because you haven't changed the inside. Changing the outside is helpful, and God will often move us to help us change. But it is partaking of the Word—really studying it, meditating on it, speaking it, and living it—that brings the internal change and conforms us to the image of Jesus.

"Anyone who listens to my teaching and obeys me is wise, like a person who builds a house on solid rock. Though the rain comes in torrents and the floodwaters rise and the winds beat against that house, it won't collapse, because it is built on rock. But anyone who hears my teaching and ignores it is foolish, like a person who builds

a house on sand. When the rains and floods come and the winds beat
against that house, it will fall with a mighty crash."

MATTHEW 7:24-27 NLT

Where is the perfect place? On the rock. You come to the place of peace on the rock of God's Word. And that perfect place is not anywhere on this earth; it is inside you.

The truth is, some of the things we worry about are going to happen in our lives. We live in a fallen world with a devil and demons and a lot of people who are moved by wickedness. However, if we build our lives upon the rock of God's Word, then whatever comes—floods, rain, tornadoes, hurricanes— our lives will still be standing when it's over.

The wind and the floods and the rain happen in all of our lives, but why is it that one will be overtaken by it and another walks away free? It's because of where we built our house and what it is made of. Our house is built by our thoughts. The perfect place of peace that sustains us through adversity is on the inside of us.

Proverbs 23:7 says, "For as he thinks in his heart, so is he." When you close your eyes, if all you see is turmoil, pain, your failures, and everything around you going down; then your house will fall. If you are continually focused on anything and everything that can go wrong, you become a ball of worry. But if you continually focus on God's promises and His Word, you will be full of faith. You won't be afraid of the storms; and when they come, you'll stand strong in peace.

How do we face the issues of terror confronting us today and come to the place of peace? By knowing the Prince of Peace, by taking the Bible internally, by choosing to believe what God says, by speaking what God says (especially to ourselves), and by staying in the perfect place of peace—peace of mind and heart, peace on the inside.

1 4

Our Inheritance of Peace

Therefore being justified by faith, we have peace with God through our Lord Jesus Christ.

ROMANS 5:1

When we were born again, we were justified, or made right with God, through faith. The inheritance we received through the last will and testament of Jesus, the covenant made in His blood, is peace. We inherit the peace of God that passes all understanding.

Peace I leave with you, my peace I give unto you: not as the world giveth, give I unto you. Let not your heart be troubled, neither let it be afraid.

JOHN 14:27

The way the world gives peace is the temporary absence of turbulence, the temporary absence of problems. That's the world's peace. But the peace we inherit through Jesus Christ is a lasting, permanent peace that sticks with us no matter what is going on around us, no matter what is happening to us. God's perfect peace is freedom from disturbance and agitation on the inside, a state of quiet tranquility within.

THE NUMBER ONE REASON WE DON'T HAVE PEACE

What is the number one reason that we are without peace? We don't trust God. And when we don't trust God we fall into worry, fear, apprehension, and anxiety. Fear is proof that we do not trust God. Fear is proof that we are not taking in God's Word and walking in God's Spirit. The fruit of the Spirit is love, joy, peace, and so on. Therefore, fear is proof that I am allowing something other than the Holy Spirit to bear fruit in my life.

Let not your heart be troubled: ye believe in God, believe also in me.

JOHN 14:1

Jesus told us several times to not let our hearts be troubled. Do not. Do not. That means do not let yourself focus on things that cause worry. Focus on the things that are established as truth in God's Word, the things that will last forever and keep you strong through any trial. Do not allow your mind to go into a pattern of wild, undisciplined thinking. Instead, you must focus on God's Word. Whatever you focus on is what you draw to yourself. It is what becomes real in your life.

So then faith cometh by hearing, and hearing by the word of God.

ROMANS 10:17

When you focus on God's Word you bring faith into your life. When you focus on everything that worries you, you bring fear into your life. Do you see how that works? Reading, studying, and meditating God's Word is like stopping by the filling station every day to make sure you have a full tank of gas. When you stop by the Bible every day, you fill your heart up with faith, hope, love, and peace. Matthew 6:34 says that sufficient to the day is the evil thereof, but also sufficient to the day is the peace thereof. You can have the peace of God all the time and throughout your day.

Thou wilt keep him in perfect peace, whose mind is stayed on thee: because he trusteth in thee.

ISAIAH 26:3

The term "perfect peace" actually means "peace peace."[1] When the Bible says something twice, that means double emphasis and double the strength. Those who keep their minds focused on God and His Word will be kept in incredible peace, the peace of the Prince of Peace Himself. Why? Because they trust in God and His Word.

FEAR IS A PERSON

Let me tell you something about fear. I have dealt with fear during a tremendous amount of my life, and fear is not a feeling. Fear is a person. It's almost like he comes and he sits down next to you. Sometimes he'll sit right on you. And when he's there, you feel him. You want to get him off you.

Fear begins with anxiety, and that anxiety begins to grow slowly, little by little, like lava making its way through our thoughts and down our body until we are gripped with fear. We associate fear with certain situations, and so we begin to build a life that avoids those situations. We stay away from things. We avoid certain people. We avoid getting into relationships because we're afraid they will hurt us. We're afraid there will be too much going on and fear will come and seize us again. We won't be able to handle it.

This kind of worry and fear is the result of a wrong self-image. It is seeing yourself incorrectly. You focus on that which is coming at you and your inability to handle it in your own strength, rather than the Holy Spirit who is alive in you, who can handle anything. You are consumed with how you are going to be able to respond to the challenges of life instead of being consumed with the life-giving Spirit of God inside you, the One who can respond to anything with overcoming power and peace. Fear is a lack of belief and trust in God's earnestness to protect you even in the midst of the storm.

THE POWER OF PERCEPTION

Here are some interesting fears that people have today. **Acoustiphobia.** Many people who come to church have acoustiphobia, which is the fear of noise. These are the people who write us a little note on their offering envelope or prayer request card, saying, "It's just too loud around here. I just can't stand the noise."

Acrophobia is the fear of heights. Many people have this fear. They'll be in New York and refuse to go out on the top deck of the Empire State Building. They won't climb a mountain. Some people can't even fly on an airplane, or if they do, they can't sit next to the window.

Agoraphobia is the fear of being in public places. A person who has this fear is a person who likes to stay home. The only time they ever feel peaceful is when they're at home. Being around a lot of people agitates them and makes them nervous and upset.

Allodoxaphobia. I'm willing to admit that I have allodoxaphobia. It's the fear of opinions. It's a horrible feeling to hear an opinion and not know if it's the truth or not. I just want people to tell me what God said about something. I don't want to get into the "they said, she said, we said, he said." I just want to hear the truth. If God told you to love people, then love them. I don't want to talk about it anymore.

Anuptaphobia is the fear of staying single. Some people want that fear! **Coulrophobia** is the fear of clowns. **Decidophobia** is the fear of making any decision whatsoever, like the scarecrow in *The Wizard of Oz*. **Genuphobia** is the fear of knees. When you have genuphobia, you know why you're afraid of knees. I have that when I sit in the front row of the church.

Eisoptrophobia is the fear of mirrors or seeing yourself in the mirror. I saw myself in the mirror the other day and cried, "Ah! Man, you're about the ugliest man in my life."

Linda walked by and said, "That's not true, darling."

I said, "I didn't ask you. I'm talking to me."

Ergasiophobia is the fear of work. **Geliophobia** is the fear of laughter. **Hippopotomonstrosesquippedaliophobia** is the fear of long words. That word is thirty-seven letters long, so just looking at it will tell you if you have that fear! **Ophthalmophobia** is the fear of being stared at. **Pentheraphobia** is the fear of your mother-in-law. **Phronemophobia** is the fear of thinking. **Pteronophobia** is the fear of being tickled with feathers.

Fear is the result of the way you perceive things. Fear isn't the way that things are. Fear is the result of the way that you perceive them, the way you think about them. If you perceive something like clowns to be dangerous and frightening, then you will back away from them. You will avoid them. You won't take your kids to the circus because you're afraid of the clowns. One of fear's goals is to get you to limit your life, to keep you from enjoying your life to the fullest.

When we live in fear we take things away in such a manner that our lives are really cornered. We live at home. We don't go out. We don't see people. We don't advance in life. We don't motivate ourselves to go beyond our own potential and draw on God's power, which is always beyond our potential. It takes faith to meet God at our point of weakness and to be filled with His strength.

SEVEN POINTS TO LIVE IN YOUR INHERITANCE OF PEACE

Following are seven points that will help you function in the midst of a storm by drawing on your inheritance of peace from the Prince of Peace. These points will help you stay in faith, fight off fear, and live in peace the way God intended you to live—no matter what is going on in your life.

1. The presence of fear is proof that you are focusing on the power of the defeated enemy—Satan. Whenever you focus on the power of that which is defeated, you destroy yourself. Satan's kingdom and all its evil can't destroy you unless you give it permission to destroy you. Worry suggests that it's going to destroy you, and it puts so much pressure on you that it causes you to be afraid. It makes your body sick. You cannot sleep. You are stressed all the time. You are at a place where you cannot handle one more thought. Eventually you come to the place where you believe the devil has got you. This is what happens when you plug into the negative thinking the devil sows in your life.

That's what happened to the children of Israel in Numbers 13:31-33, when the spies who had come back from spying out the Promised Land gave their reports. Ten of the spies gave an evil report. God called it evil because it focused on the enemy's strengths and elevated the enemy's power over God's power. The ten spies said this: "You know, the land really does flow with milk and honey. It's exactly what God said it was going to be. But you know what? The children of Anak are there. They're the sons of the giants. We can't take this land because they're stronger than we are."

Now why do you think those ten spies came back with an evil report? Why did they think the giants were stronger than they were? I'll tell you why. They had been listening to the rumors and stories about the children of Anak for so long that they were afraid of them before they even saw them. They probably were so afraid of them that when they finally saw them, their perception of them was bigger than they actually were. They said they were grasshoppers compared to the giants, and in reality, that is a gross exaggeration.

Fear only has the power that you give it. Until you heard about somebody dying from a bungee jumping accident, you did it every day. It didn't bother you. You thought it was wonderful. You had to switch legs, alternating from one leg to the other leg so one leg didn't stretch out beyond the other, but it was no big deal. Then one day they told you all the bad things that could happen to you and you stopped. Fear sat down and got you focused on the negative, so now you avoid what used to give you pleasure.

In order for you to be a grasshopper in someone's sight, you must first be a grasshopper in your own sight. In order for the defeated enemy to overtake you, you must first see it as being greater than you are in Jesus Christ. If you see yourself smaller than the challenge, you will talk yourself out of the game. You will just walk away. You'll say, "Man, that's it. I'm not going to do it. I'm not going to fight. I'm not even going to get in the game."

2. The presence of courage is the proof that your perception is right. In 1 Samuel, chapter 17, you read the famous story of David and Goliath. David's father had sent him to bring food to his brothers and cheese to his brothers' captain, who were all at war against the Philistines. While David was making his delivery, he saw and heard Goliath, the Philistine giant, come forward and challenge the Israelites. First Samuel 17:24 says, "When the Israelites saw the man, they all ran from him in great fear." Since David was standing with his brothers on the battle lines (see verses 22-23), he probably ran too. Fear can cause a herd mentality. When you listen and follow other people, you'll get scared when they get scared and run when they run.

While David was hanging out with the soldiers and his brothers, he heard some of them say, "You know, nobody could take this guy. But if someone does, the king said his family is going to be free. He said he'll never pay taxes again, he'll get to marry the king's daughter, and he'll get all kinds of stuff."

David said, "Wait a second. Tell me again. You mean if somebody whoops this giant, who has been browbeating you guys for a while, he'll get the king's daughter and all kinds of riches, and his family won't have to pay any more taxes?"

One of the men answered, "That's right."

David said, "Well, who is this uncircumcised Philistine that he would defy the armies of the living God? Who is he?"

At that, David's brother Eliab got mad at him, saying, "David, we know you are full of pride and sin. You just came here to watch the battle. You're bad."

But David was not being prideful. He was being courageous because his perception was right. Courage is the proof that David's focus was clear. He knew God's power and authority were much greater than any giant in the land. He knew that God would help him bring down the giant in the same way He had enabled David to kill the lion and the bear. He knew that He was in covenant with God, and God would defeat his enemies.

With that understanding David knew his objective. He knew his goal. He knew exactly where he was going. He knew exactly what he wanted to accomplish. Each of the other soldiers, including David's brothers, were saying, "Well, even though I could be the king's son-in-law, my family could be free of taxes forever, and I'd get all this wealth; I'm more scared of Goliath than I am of taxes."

We all know how the story ends. David picked up five smooth stones from a brook, put the first stone in his sling, and brought Goliath down on the first try. Then he marched over to the giant, picked up his massive sword, and chopped the giant's head off with his own weapon. David's courage proved that of all the soldiers, he had the right perception!

3. Peace is not the absence of trouble; it is the awareness of God's presence. God's peace doesn't mean the absence of trouble. One of the things believers think is, *If God really loves me, how come all of these terrible things are going on in my life?* They have this idea that just because they're children of God, they're not going to have any trouble. But let's see what the Bible really says about trouble.

> *Those who live in the shelter of the Most High will find rest in the shadow of the Almighty.*
>
> *This I declare of the LORD: He alone is my refuge, my place of safety; he is my God, and I am trusting him.*
>
> *The LORD says, "I will rescue those who love me. I will protect those who trust in my name.*
>
> PSALM 91:1,2,14 NLT

The psalmist writes that God is his place of safety. You have to understand that peace is not the absence of trouble but the awareness that God is there no matter what. Personally, I make sure God is busy in my life. I cry out to Him, "Oh, God, can't You see what's happening to me? Put a rope around my leg. Pull me out of this, in the name of Jesus!" I do this because He said He would rescue those who love Him, and I love Him.

> *When they call on me, I will answer; I will be with them in trouble. I will rescue them and honor them.*
>
> *I will satisfy them with a long life and give them my salvation.*
>
> PSALM 91:15,16 NLT

Knowing that God is with us wherever we go and in whatever situation we find ourselves makes the difference between living a life filled with worry and living a life filled with peace.

4. Peace is experienced when you fix your thoughts on God. In Isaiah 26:3 NLT, the Bible says, "You will keep in perfect peace all who trust in you, whose thoughts are fixed on you!" Mind fixation upon God is proof of your trust in Him. What you fix your mind on is what you're trusting. If you fix your thoughts on gloom and doom, then gloom and doom is what you are trusting in. If you fix your thoughts on the promises of God, then you are trusting in the promises of God. So peace is experienced by those who fix their thoughts on God.

All the children of God are given the inheritance of perfect peace. Ephesians 6:15 says that our feet are shod with the gospel of peace. Philippians 4:7 says that the peace of God keeps our hearts and minds, no matter where we are or what we're doing. And Philippians 4:9 says that the God of peace is with us always. When you focus on God, you are focusing on peace because He is peace.

5. Meditation on who you are in Christ will end all emotional unrest. You are not to meditate on who you were or who you want to be. You are to meditate on who you are right now in Jesus Christ, and this will end all sorts of emotional unrest and bring you right into your inheritance of peace. For example, you are righteous through the blood of Jesus, and in Isaiah 32:17 it says, "And the work of righteousness shall be peace; and the effect of righteousness quietness and assurance for ever." The work of righteousness will be peace.

As you go throughout your day doing the work of righteousness, serving and worshiping God and doing all things as unto the Lord, you will walk in peace. Why? Because you cannot do the work of righteousness without knowing who you are in Jesus Christ.

6. Surrendering to God ignites peace within you. If you haven't already given your entire heart and being to God, I want to encourage you to fully surrender to Him. Then, when it comes to living your daily life, you surrender to what God's Word says. When it comes to everything about who you are, you surrender to what God's Word says. When everything that concerns you—including yourself—belongs completely to God, you have no worries. He is in control and He loves you. People will look at you and ask, "What do you think might happen?" And you are going to tell them that you don't care. "Yeah, but don't you think God wants you to care?"

"Well, His Word says that I'm to cast all my cares on Him, so that's what I'm doing." When you have no cares, you have no worries; and when you have no worries, you are walking in your inheritance of peace.

"Yeah, but don't you think you ought to be worried about this?"

"No, He told me:

> *Don't worry about anything; instead, pray about everything. Tell God what you need, and thank him for all he has done. If you do this, you will experience God's peace, which is far more wonderful than the human mind can understand. His peace will guard your hearts and minds as you live in Christ Jesus.*
>
> PHILIPPIANS 4:6,7 NLT

Surrendering your entire life to God, casting all your cares on Him and praying instead of worrying will keep you in God's peace.

7. Embracing God's thoughts expels all fear. "God, what do You think about this? How do You feel about this?" I cannot be any more frank or open with you than this: Life apart from knowing what God thinks is empty and frightening. In Psalm 119:165, the psalmist wrote, "Great peace have they which love thy law [God's Word]: and nothing shall offend them." When we embrace God's Word we are embracing His thoughts, and God does not think in terms of worry, fear, doubt, apprehension, and anxiety. God's thoughts are filled with peace.

To eradicate all worry and fear from your life, you must begin to draw upon the inheritance God has given you in Christ, this vast reservoir of peace. You do that by having the right perception of your situation, emphasizing God's role and minimizing the devil's role, knowing who you are in Him, surrendering your whole heart to Him, and thinking and acting like Him. And you must always remember that being His child does not mean the absence of trouble but the presence of peace in the midst of trouble.

To fully appreciate and walk in our inheritance of peace through Christ Jesus is one of the most amazing parts of the Christian life. We are given this incredible inheritance when we are born again, but too few of us really tap into the depth of it. In our world today, if we begin to really walk in our inheritance of peace, those who are living apart from God and walking in fear will turn to us for the answer. Walking in our inheritance of peace not only makes our lives more full and joyful, it also opens the door to tell the lost about the Prince of Peace.

1 5

Sustaining Peace

*And the peace of God, which passeth all understanding, shall
keep your hearts and minds through Christ Jesus.*

PHILIPPIANS 4:7

How do we come to the point in our lives when we can
begin to walk into rooms and not be worried? Wouldn't it be
nice to be so peaceful that no one and nothing could agitate us
anymore? People would think we were on some new divine
drug. The *No Worries* drug.

When there's a lack of peace there's a lack of safety. Each of
us is searching for that place of peace where we can relax and
feel safe. The truth is, we will never find that perfect place in
the natural. Even the most beautiful places on earth are subject
to violent storms. No, this place of peace has to be a place in
our hearts. Then, no matter who we are with or where we are
or what we are doing—we are in that place of perfect peace.

Do you know that you can walk around for days with a lack
of peace and not even realize it? You don't know what's wrong
with you. On the other hand, sometimes you are walking in
peace when someone else will walk in and give you an uneasy
feeling. You feel like you've got to be on your guard every time
they're around. You can see their wheels turning, and you know
it's going to cost you some peace of mind to talk to them.

These people do nothing but try to take away your peace and get you worried about something. You don't feel safe with them. But I figured out a long time ago that they weren't the problem; I was the problem. I didn't have enough peace inside me to feel safe with them, so I worried about them.

The Bible addresses this in Luke 10, when Jesus is visiting His good friends Lazarus, Mary, and Martha in Bethany. Many believe that this was Jesus' favorite hangout, and that this family was some of His closest friends. As we well know, however, Martha got totally worried about feeding everyone, and Jesus had to correct her for worrying so much.

THE WORD SUSTAINS PEACE

Isn't it funny that when somebody doesn't have peace in their life, everything that concerns them becomes a huge issue. They begin to worry about everything. Not only was Martha worried about feeding everyone, but she also became worried that Mary was not doing what she should be doing—helping her! That's why Jesus said to her in Luke 10:41, "Martha, Martha, thou art careful and troubled about *many* things."

When we don't deal with our lack of peace, everything becomes a worry to us. And what Jesus told Martha was what He would tell us today with all our worries. In Luke 10:42 He said, "But one thing is needful: and Mary hath chosen that good part, which shall not be taken away from her." Jesus was referring to the fact that Mary was sitting at His feet listening to the Word of God. This is the "good part" that cannot be taken away from us. The Word of God gives us a peace that passes all understanding and that cannot be taken away from us.

Jesus told Martha that she needed to drive out her worries with the Word of God. Only then would she experience a peace that could not be shaken, no matter what she was facing in life.

And then she would no longer be worried about dinner or about Mary. Martha was not bothered because she had too much to do in too little time with too little help. She was bothered because she wasn't spending any time in the Word.

Before I understood this, I had a lot of problems with being able to keep my word when it came to social commitments. Linda and I would accept an invitation to have dinner with some people, and when the time came I would freak out. I'm not tremendously social to begin with. I don't like crowds. I don't feel like I communicate very well. And I'm not very confident in a group of people. So halfway to the party, we'd be driving along and I would say, "That's it. I'm going home." Or if Linda did manage to get me there, I'd hide somewhere. I have been found in a closet more than once! It's always so exciting when someone opens the door, sees you, and you go, "Hi there," like what you're doing is normal.

Finally I had to deal with this worry that I just couldn't be around people in a social situation. I took Jesus' advice to Martha to heart and decided that I couldn't go out to do anything with anybody until I first spent time with God in His Word. Before going out, I would go into my office and shut the door. I would read and study the Word and pray until I had the confidence in God and the inner peace I needed to be able to be with people in a social situation. The key to sustaining inner peace is staying close to God and His Word.

I know that when I have no peace in my life I am not spending enough time in the Word of God. When I repeatedly do not choose the better part, which is sitting at Jesus' feet and learning of Him, I worry about everything and become a wreck. I cannot live without the sustaining peace that comes from the Word of God.

Colossians 3:15 WUEST says, "And the peace of Christ, let it be acting as an umpire in your hearts." The *King James Version* says, "And let the peace of God rule in your hearts." You see, until I come to the place where the peace of God is the umpire of my life, where peace rules and calls the shots, then I can't start my day. I've started too many days without it, and it messes up everything!

FOUR KEYS TO SUSTAINING PEACE

Here are a few of the specific things I do to sustain the peace of God in my life.

1. I'm always conscious of the fact that Jesus paid the price for my peace. When you notice that you don't have peace in your life, you'll begin to worry that you did something wrong. "What did I do wrong?" But wait a minute. If God was going to get you for doing something wrong, why are you still breathing? Why did He let you get out of bed this morning? He'd have shot you before you opened your eyes because He's perfect and you aren't.

The fact that God is perfect and you are not is only true in your flesh, however. Jesus paid the price for your sin, and when God sees you He sees a sinless, perfect Jesus person. All of this is revealed clearly in the book of Isaiah.

> *Surely he hath borne our griefs, and carried our sorrows: yet we did esteem him stricken, smitten of God, and afflicted.*
>
> *But he was wounded for our transgressions, he was bruised for our iniquities: the chastisement of our peace was upon him; and with his stripes we are healed.*
>
> ISAIAH 53:4,5

You must realize that Jesus has paid the price for your sin so that perfect peace could be yours. In order to sustain peace you first must understand the origin and source of that peace. Jesus is the source of your peace. Ephesians 2:14 says that Jesus is our peace because His death and resurrection are the reason we have peace.

2. I remember Jesus gave me His peace. After Jesus paid for my peace, He gave it to me. He said these words in John 14:27: "Peace I leave with you, my peace I give unto you: not as the world giveth, give I unto you. Let not your heart be troubled, neither let it be afraid." Sometimes I say to myself over and over, "Don't be troubled. Don't be afraid." And I continually remind myself that Jesus not only paid for my peace with His precious blood, but then He gave me His peace.

Jesus didn't say, "I've given you My peace when everything's just wonderful at your house." He said, "I gave you My peace for when everything's rotten as well as when everything's great." You have His peace inside you no matter what's taking place in your life—not because you're so good and perfect, but because He gave it to you.

3. I focus on God. There are so many things I can be worrying about, and when I lose my sense of inner peace I know that I have lost focus—my focus on God.

Ask yourself right now if you're focusing on God and how great He is, or if you're focusing on what you're worrying about and how big it is. Or maybe you're concerned about too many things. You're running in the proverbial hither, thither, and yon. You're off doing everything under the sun and so you're accomplishing nothing. Spinning your wheels. Why? Because you've broken focus. When you lose focus, you lose everything. Proverbs 29:18 says that when there is no vision (focus on what God wants) then we perish. Perish means perish! You're lost and destroyed. You're going nowhere and your destination is ruin.

You can only sustain peace and defeat all your worries if you stay focused on God, on the fact that Jesus paid for peace and then gave it to you, on His will, and on who He created you to be in Him. Without that vision always before you, you will perish. The reason many believers don't feel any peace is because even though they know that Jesus paid for it and gave it to them, they listen to every voice that wants to pull them away from Him. They don't stay focused on Him. Isaiah 26:3 says, "Thou wilt keep him in perfect peace, whose mind is stayed on thee: because he trusteth in thee."

The peace Jesus paid for and gave to you is "perfect peace." We are not talking about a half-baked, temporary, incomplete peace. We are talking about a peace that passes your human understanding because it stays with you no matter what happens. There is no flaw in God's peace, and it is the ultimate and best peace because it comes from above. He gives us *His* peace. This is the ultimate peace of the universe.

When you stay focused on Him, you sustain His peace within you. When you don't feel His peace, it's not because it leaves you, but because you left it by focusing on other things. You got caught up in your worries and forgot the reservoir of peace inside you that was all about Him and who He is to you. He will keep you. He will protect you and guard you. He is faithful and just and loving. He can be trusted.

When your heart and mind are fully connected and focused on Him, His peace is ruling your heart and mind. "Yeah, but what if?" Don't "what if" anything! "If" doesn't mean a thing in the kingdom of God because all of God's promises are yes and amen to those who believe and trust Him. He keeps you in perfect peace.

4. I meditate on the Word of God for extended periods of time. If I realize that I have no peace or have become unsettled or worried about something, I immediately go to God's Word and start meditating on it.

The moment you realize you're off track, you have to pull yourself back on track. You just reel yourself back in to God's safe harbor. One of the reasons you miss a lot of peace in your life is that you allow yourself to slowly drift away from God's Word. It happens a little at a time, so you don't realize how far you're getting from Him and the truth.

Then one day, maybe months or years down the line, you wake up to the fact that your life is a total mess and you have no peace. When you sit down with God and His Word and get your brain cleared of all the confusion, you realize that it all started the day you decided not to read and meditate on the Word. You can trace the source of your present problems and lack of peace back to that decision not to stay committed to the Word of God.

In the fourth chapter of Proverbs, David sets his son, Solomon, straight in the same way God sets us straight.

> *My son, attend to my words; incline thine ear unto my sayings.*
>
> *Let them not depart from thine eyes; keep them in the midst of thine heart.*
>
> *For they are life unto those that find them, and health to all their flesh.*
>
> PROVERBS 4:20-22

David was saying, "Solomon, quit looking around. You bend your ear when I speak, not when your thoughts are telling you other things. Pay attention to what I'm saying." God's saying the same thing to us as He did to Joshua.

> *This book of the law shall not depart out of thy mouth; but thou shalt meditate therein day and night, that thou mayest observe to do according to all that is written therein: for then thou shalt make thy way prosperous, and then thou shalt have good success.*
>
> JOSHUA 1:8

You ought to go to bed at night with a neon sign of 1 Peter 2:24 in the back of your eyelids: "Who his own self bare our sins in his own body on the tree, that we, being dead to sins, should live unto righteousness: by whose stripes ye were healed." Go to sleep playing the Scriptures in your mind. Wake up listening to them in the morning. In the middle of the night you are listening. You're attending.

You see, if you spend time during the day listening to teaching tapes about the Word, reading and studying the Word, and then meditating on the Word; when you turn the tapes off and shut the books, the Word is still working in your mind and heart. You can still hear it and see it. And that's when the Word begins to guide you so that you make the right decisions and have the "good success" God promised you.

There's no greater success than living in the peace of God. When you're walking in the peace of God you don't care what neighborhood you're walking through. All you care about is doing what He's called you to do. You don't worry about the possible dangers and setbacks because His peace rules your heart and mind.

Now I have to deal with something here. You cannot do this backwards. You cannot get religious and try to prove you have peace by doing something God has not told you to do. "Well, I'm going to prove to you that I've got peace in my life and go to the dangerous part of town to talk to people about Jesus." No! That is a sure way to NOT have good success. You are acting in pride and not in peace or faith. The person who does this has no peace and is trying to prove they have peace by doing a foolish thing.

If you have no peace, you need to get in God's Word and start meditating it day and night before you do anything. Faith comes by hearing and hearing by the Word of God, so then you can go out with faith as well as peace.

THE STRATEGIC POWER OF SUSTAINING PEACE

Sustaining peace in your life is a powerful force for the devil, the world, and your flesh to reckon with! When you understanding how strategic the peace that passes all understanding is to your success as a believer in Jesus Christ, you will do everything you know to sustain it. I believe that is why Ephesians 6:15 says that our feet are shod with the gospel of peace. The Good News that we carry to the world is a message of peace.

1 6

Overcoming Anxiety and Terror

Anxiety in the heart of man causes depression, But a good word makes it glad.

PROVERBS 12:5 NKJV

If ever we needed to hear a good word to stay glad about life it is in today's world. People all over the world are riddled with anxiety and worry because of the War on Terror. But how does that affect us as believers? The Bible tells us that we are overcomers, but just how are we supposed to overcome anxiety and terror?

Anxiety lets us know that it is time to get rid of some bad habits of thinking, speaking, and behaving before it is too late and we fall into full-blown depression. This can be quite disabling, so it is important for us to understand and defeat anxiety in our lives.

THE CHARACTERISTICS OF ANXIETY AND TERROR

Generally, anxiety is characterized by excessive worry about a number of ordinary events or activities such as our job, our school, our marriage, our children, our relatives, our health, our safety, and so on. In order for worrying to become anxiety, we must have been worrying about the same things for a period of time.

Anxiety is somewhat more acute than worry. Worry can be just for a moment. Anxiety is something that continues to nag at us. It brings out funny behavior and feelings in degrees over time. These behaviors and feelings include being on edge, fatigue, difficulty concentrating, irritability, muscle tension, headaches and other physical aches and pains, and not being able to sleep.

A person who deals with anxiety is a person who really doesn't care very much about what's going on in the lives of others because it is all they can do to survive each day. They think about themselves most of the time and look at life from the perspective of, "How is this going to affect me? Can I take this? What am I going to get out of this? Is this worth it?" Their relationships all have to do with, "Is this person going to be good for me? Is this person going to cause me more trouble?"

Those who are riddled with anxiety make commitments and then don't fulfill them. They're individuals who will make appointments to meet people and then not show up. Anxiety drives them to be unfaithful, and that causes even more anxiety, especially if they are Christians and know better. Anxiety causes people to be very self-centered. They think that the whole world is against them and closing in on them quicker than they can run away from it.

Now what if we keep on worrying and the anxiety builds and builds? Then we enter into terror. Terror is fear that grips our souls so tightly that it paralyzes us. We are living in a time where terror and terrorists are a continuous, daily fact of life. Therefore, it is vital that the body of Christ knows how to defeat terror.

How do you overcome terror in your life? How do you get rid of paralyzing fear? How do you deal with the pressure of knowing any minute a terrorist could blow up your children's school, the building where you work, or the grocery store where you go to pick up some milk? How do you deal with all the feelings of dread and the constant "what ifs" that the media throw at you?

THE ULTIMATE "WHAT IF"

First, let's take a good look at the ultimate "what if" scenario. What if I were to tell you that the terrorist behind all other terrorist activities, the guy who had trained every other terrorist who trained other terrorists, was now in solitary confinement and powerless? That would be wonderful, wouldn't it? The truth of the matter is that it's already happened—and I'm not referring to the death of Yassar Arafat, the father of modern terrorism.

> *Forasmuch then as the children are partakers of flesh and blood, he also himself likewise took part of the same; that through death he might destroy him that had the power of death, that is, the devil;*
>
> *And deliver them who through fear of death were all their lifetime subject to bondage.*
>
> HEBREWS 2:15,16

The greatest terrorist of all time was defeated by Jesus Christ. People are bound by fear their entire lives if they do not get set free by Jesus Christ. Let's look at one big fear they live with: the fear of man. The Bible calls these people "menpleasers."

> *Servants, be obedient to them that are your masters according to the flesh, with fear and trembling, in singleness of your heart, as unto Christ;*
>
> *Not with eyeservice, as menpleasers; but as the servants of Christ, doing the will of God from the heart;*
>
> *With good will doing service, as to the Lord, and not to men:*

Knowing that whatsoever good thing any man doeth, the same shall he receive of the Lord, whether he be bond or free.

EPHESIANS 6:5-8

For do I now persuade men, or God? or do I seek to please men? for if I yet pleased men, I should not be the servant of Christ.

GALATIANS 1:10

When you become a men-pleaser you do everything you can do to please people. You hate conflict or the thought of an argument or a disagreement. You just want everybody to be happy, so you become somewhat of a UN peacekeeper. This is a false peacekeeper because you will sacrifice what is right for keeping the peace. You will not pay the price for God's Word, which is righteous and just, but say or do whatever someone wants you to say or do to keep a fragile peace.

Do you know what happens to false peacekeepers? They are the ones who get shot and beat up because they don't know how to fight. They've never learned because they were too frightened of conflict to even entertain the idea of learning to defend themselves from evil. Their mantra is, "Can't we all be friends? Can't we all just love one another?"

The idea that we should all be able to get along and love one another is a false perception of human nature and the world, and it leads to total destruction. Jesus often referred to "the wicked." Some people are under Satan's influence and want to do nothing but steal, kill, and destroy. If you don't fight them, you will either join them or be destroyed by them.

Think not that I am come to send peace on earth: I came not to send peace, but a sword.

MATTHEW 10:34

Jesus also said that if we lived our lives for Him, it would cause conflict. He knew the earth was filled with the enemies of

God. He knew that those who followed God would have to deal with conflict, affliction, and warfare—spiritual and natural. We have seen in the past three chapters that the peace Jesus brought was the *inner peace* we have to go through conflict, affliction, and warfare. Through the blood of Jesus we have peace with God forever, so we have no worries on the inside about what tomorrow may bring.

ENFORCE THE TERRORIST'S DEFEAT

When Jesus destroyed the power of the devil, He gave believers authority over the enemy of their souls. The only one who can put me back in bondage to fear is me. If I don't use the authority in the name and blood of Jesus that He gave to me, if I don't enforce Jesus' defeat of this original terrorist, then I am allowing him to terrorize me.

This is how the devil terrorizes us. He gets to know us and then he takes advantage of our weaknesses. He tells us we can't do anything because we'll fail. He tells us to stay away from people and close relationships because we'll be controlled, manipulated, and hurt. He points out every fault and flaw in our lives. He lists all the terrible things that can happen to us if we get out of bed. Then he lists the terrible things that can happen if we don't get out of bed! We back up and back up until finally we're pressed against the wall, paralyzed in confusion. Our bodies are all worn out, we have no more money, and the whole world is a dark, scary place.

Every human being has to deal with worry, fear, and terror. In case you think I'm just talking about a few strange people in the world, let me quote a few who have dealt with terror. Throughout time there have been people who have been so bound by fear that it caused them to write about it.

You gain strength, courage, and confidence by every experience in which you really stop to look fear in the face. You must do the thing which you think you cannot do.

ELEANOR ROOSEVELT

Anxiety is a thin stream of fear trickling throughout the mind. If encouraged, it cuts a channel into which all other thoughts are drained.

ROBERT ALLEN BLOCK

Fear cuts a rut inside us. It becomes a ditch in our lives that we fall into no matter how hard we try not to. It speaks to us in the morning and at night. And all other thoughts pass through this rut, this ditch of fear. Everything we think is colored by fear, and so everything we say and do is driven by fear.

When we see everything from the perspective of fear, we decide we can't do certain things, we can't be with certain people, we can't go to certain places, and any kind of change from our set routine becomes a nightmare. Terror is a blockage in the heart to your walk with God. It puts you in bondage to keep you from freely loving and serving Him.

Terror creates a spiritual heart attack that the medical community calls an anxiety attack or panic attack. Those of us who have experienced them know that everything goes on red alert in your mind and body. Your heart's racing, your mind is out of control, nothing makes any sense, and you think you have no future. It's all over and you don't know if you're ever going to be free. It can come on you in the middle of the night or in the middle of the day. But it comes without warning. You begin to sweat profusely. Many times you have all of the symptoms of a heart attack, so you rush to the hospital, only to be told that you are suffering from acute anxiety.

You see, the spirit of fear doesn't necessarily go away just because you get saved. That can happen, like when some drug addicts get saved and are immediately delivered. But in most cases the habits and problems you had before you were saved are still there to be dealt with after you're saved. And the spirit of fear has usually programmed your mind and body so well that it doesn't take much to get the whole panic attack syndrome going.

The first thing you have to do is face the fact that you have a problem. You see you can only avoid facing your enemy for so long. There will be a day when you have to face him, and the best time to face an enemy is when he is his smallest. And the enemy is smallest until you allow him to talk to you. He can convince you that he's Godzilla when he's really only Adam Ant!

Marilyn Ferguson said these words: "Ultimately we know deeply that the other side of every fear is freedom." This means that if you face your worry, anxiety, fear, and terror, you will reach a point where you will enter a new and bigger place of freedom to know God, worship Him, and serve Him.

VITAL FACTS TO GET FREE AND STAY FREE

In my years of overcoming anxiety and terror, I have discovered certain facts that have enabled me to keep a godly perspective and become more and more free.

1. Fear was born in the Garden. In the book of Genesis we have the story of what happened when Adam and Eve ate the fruit of the tree God had told them not to eat from, the tree of the knowledge of good and evil.

> *And when the woman saw that the tree was good for food, and that it was pleasant to the eyes, and a tree to be desired to make one wise, she took of the fruit thereof, and did eat, and gave also unto her husband with her; and he did eat.*

And the eyes of them both were opened, and they knew that they were naked; and they sewed fig leaves together, and made themselves aprons.

And they heard the voice of the LORD God walking in the garden in the cool of the day: and Adam and his wife hid themselves from the presence of the LORD God amongst the trees of the garden.

And the LORD God called unto Adam, and said unto him, Where art thou?

And he said, I heard thy voice in the garden, and I was afraid, because I was naked; and I hid myself.

And he said, Who told thee that thou wast naked? Hast thou eaten of the tree, whereof I commanded thee that thou shouldest not eat?

And the man said, The woman whom thou gavest to be with me, she gave me of the tree, and I did eat.

And the LORD God said unto the woman, What is this that thou hast done? And the woman said, The serpent beguiled me, and I did eat.

GENESIS 3:6-13

God asked Adam, "Did you eat something that you shouldn't have eaten?" And Adam said that he was afraid of God because he was naked, and so he hid from God. The human race became afraid of God and everything else in the world. Fear was born in the Garden.

2. Fear rules in the hearts of people apart from Jesus Christ. We need to come to grips with the fact that without Jesus fear rules in people's lives. That's what causes people to make many of the decisions they make. They're fear-driven. When an individual is fear-driven, they have faith in something that hasn't happened and probably will not happen. All their decisions are made from a perspective of fear. Remember, once that ditch of fear is established, every other thought goes down the fear track.

Do you understand the importance of this fact? As believers in this world, we deal with fear every day. We have to look in its face every day and tell it that we are no longer in bondage to it. Instead of giving place to the devil, we meditate and confess Hebrews 2:15 that says we are no longer subject to the devil, who kept us in bondage to fear before we became children of God.

3. Fear can rule even in the life of a minister. Fear can rule in the life of someone who has the call of God on their life. I was washing my hands in a restroom one day when a minister who had taught me a tremendous amount about faith hit the door so hard that he knocked it against the wall. He had this frightened look on his face and ran from stall to stall looking for his wallet. I just thought, *Are you gonna teach me about faith now?*

Yes, even ministers of the gospel, mighty men of faith, have to defeat terror in their lives. In 2 Timothy 1:8 the Bible tells us, "Be not thou therefore ashamed of the testimony of our Lord, nor of me his prisoner: but be thou partaker of the afflictions of the gospel according to the power of God." Paul is telling Timothy not to be ashamed of the gospel or of him.

Why was Timothy afraid? Because the apostle Paul kept getting him in trouble. Every time Timothy turned around Paul would shoot his mouth off and get beat up. Now Paul was in jail, and none of Paul's enemies could get to him. So they beat up Timothy because he was associated with Paul. That's why Paul is telling Timothy not to be ashamed of preaching the gospel or being associated with him.

Paul also exhorted Timothy not to be afraid of the afflictions of the gospel, and he reminded him that we endure these afflictions through the power of God, not in our own strength. Now maybe you're saying, "I want the victorious gospel. I don't want to hear this stuff about being afflicted. I want the blessed gospel. I want the triumphant gospel." Well, that's what I'm giving you! You can't be victorious, blessed, and triumphant without overcoming your worries, fears, and the terror of the day.

What we see from this passage of Scripture is that if Paul and Timothy had to deal with fear and terror, then all ministers of the gospel will have to deal with it to one degree or another—and every believer is a minister of reconciliation. The important thing all of us must remember is that Jesus has already overcome terror. First John 4:4 says, "Ye are of God, little children, and have overcome them: because greater is he that is in you, than he that is in the world."

4. Faith cannot work in a fear-filled heart. In the book of Mark, chapter 5, it gives us the story of Jairus. He came to Jesus in desperation because his little daughter was at the point of death.

> *And, behold, there cometh one of the rulers of the synagogue, Jairus by name; and when he saw him, he fell at his feet,*
>
> *And besought him greatly, saying, My little daughter lieth at the point of death: I pray thee, come and lay thy hands on her, that she may be healed; and she shall live.*
>
> *And Jesus went with him; and much people followed him, and thronged him.*
>
> MARK 5:22-24

Jairus is hopeful because Jesus is on the way to heal his daughter, but then a tremendous crowd surrounds them. Every second counts at this point, so Jairus's heart is racing. He must get Jesus to his daughter before she dies. The crowd is causing him serious problems, and if that isn't enough, a pushy woman with an issue of blood gets in the way. She crawls on the ground through the crowd and finally grabs the hem of Jesus' garment, and that stops the whole procession.

Jesus comes to a halt and says, "Who touched Me?" And all of His disciples look at Him like He's crazy.

"What do You mean, 'Who touched Me?' There are fifteen people touching You right now and hundreds pressing in on You."

> And Jesus, immediately knowing in himself that virtue had gone out of him, turned him about in the press, and said, Who touched my clothes?
>
> And his disciples said unto him, Thou seest the multitude thronging thee, and sayest thou, Who touched me?
>
> And he looked round about to see her that had done this thing.
>
> But the woman fearing and trembling, knowing what was done in her, came and fell down before him, and told him all the truth.
>
> And he said unto her, Daughter, thy faith hath made thee whole; go in peace, and be whole of thy plague.
>
> MARK 5:30-34

Jesus felt someone draw healing from Him, someone who had incredible faith in Him. That's why He stopped and turned to find out who it was. When He did that, the woman got scared because she was not supposed to be there. Her issue of blood made her unclean, and she shouldn't have been in public. Touching Jesus was even worse. But Jesus assured her that He was pleased with her faith in Him, that her faith in Him had healed her. She had refused to allow the terror of fearing death rule her heart. Instead, she filled her heart with faith that Jesus could set her free when she touched Him. But the woman with the issue of blood is not the only one who overcomes terror with faith in Jesus.

> While he yet spake, there came from the ruler of the synagogue's house certain which said, Thy daughter is dead: why troublest thou the Master any further?
>
> As soon as Jesus heard the word that was spoken, he saith unto the ruler of the synagogue, Be not afraid, only believe.

And he suffered no man to follow him, save Peter, and James, and John the brother of James.

And he cometh to the house of the ruler of the synagogue, and seeth the tumult, and them that wept and wailed greatly.

And when he was come in, he saith unto them, Why make ye this ado, and weep? the damsel is not dead, but sleepeth.

And they laughed him to scorn. But when he had put them all out, he taketh the father and the mother of the damsel, and them that were with him, and entereth in where the damsel was lying.

And he took the damsel by the hand, and said unto her, Talitha cumi; which is, being interpreted, Damsel, I say unto thee, arise.

And straightway the damsel arose, and walked; for she was of the age of twelve years. And they were astonished with a great astonishment.

MARK 5:35-42

While Jesus was talking to the woman who had been healed from the issue of blood, Jairus's worst fears were realized. His servant arrived and said that his daughter had died. It was too late. But before Jairus could begin mourning, Jesus told him not to be afraid and to continue to believe and have faith. The Bible doesn't say so, but it seems pretty obvious that Jairus decided to have faith in Jesus instead of giving up. Why? Because Jesus went straight to his daughter's bedside and raised her from the dead.

Your heart cannot be filled with fear when you believe the Word of God.

5. Let Jesus' words talk to you, not fear-filled words. Jairus let the words of Jesus fill his heart instead of worrying words of fear and terror. And that's what you need to do. Don't let terror talk to you. Whatever battle you are fighting, in the beginning it is easy to throw off evil thoughts of worry, fear, and terror. But as you get closer and closer to winning the battle, it will seem like every demon in hell is sitting on your shoulder trying to terrify you and get you to quit in discouragement and fear.

We often lose it when we're just about to get where we want to go because fear brings together all of its resources when it knows we are about to win the battle. When we first step out in faith fear shows up, but we defeat it and it goes away for a while. Then, just when we are close to total victory, every fear-driving devil shows up. We feel like a beat-up man by the side of the road and the vultures are circling, knowing how weak and vulnerable we are. This is the most critical time in our fight to freedom because this is when most people give up and give in to terror—at the point they are about to break through!

What I'm telling you is that it is always darkest just before the dawn. You cannot give up! And the way you keep from giving up and giving into terror is by listening to what Jesus tells you in His Word instead of what the vulture-demons of fear are telling you.

6. You must fight for you. Let me tell you something: God never lets anybody get your trophy for you. You have to win your battle. No one can do it for you. Remember, the devil does everything he can do to wear you down because you are the only one who can decide to be defeated. The devil cannot beat you if you decide to have faith in Jesus and to not give up until you break through into freedom and blessing. Jesus already destroyed Satan and took the keys of death and the grave from him. So Satan can only terrorize you if you let him.

One of the ways you get the devil to back off with his terror tactics is by continually reminding yourself of the truth: the devil is a liar! He never told the truth; he's not going to tell the truth today or tomorrow or next week or next month. If you persist in standing up to him and refuse his lying thoughts of terror, you will win.

You also must have wisdom to fight well. When you begin to muster all of your strength to defeat something that has been plaguing you, you have to pace yourself to know when to rest in the Lord and gain His strength and when to get out there and fight. You need those times with the Lord to be spiritually ready to handle the issue and to endure the battle, no matter how long it takes. You cannot just give it a swipe every once in a while. That will not make it go away. You must focus on it and refuse to let go until it is gone.

You can only get rid of what you are unwilling to tolerate. I don't tolerate certain issues in my life. I don't tolerate low self-esteem. I don't tolerate bad attitudes. And I refuse to tolerate fear and terror anymore. But if you begin to tolerate these things, you will go one step further and want others to believe God for you instead of doing it yourself. This places you in a very vulnerable position. You are so afraid and so oppressed that you want someone else to believe God for you. You want them to get into the Word and pray for you.

In Genesis, chapter 12, God tells Abram to get out of his father's house, leave his kindred and his nation, and go to a land he's never been before. When Abram comes to Egypt he is afraid of what will happen to him if they see how beautiful Sarai, his wife, is. He is afraid they will kill him to get her, so he tells everyone that they are brother and sister.

As it turns out, the men notice how gorgeous Sarai is and take her into the harem of the king, Abimelech. Abimelech goes to sleep that night, and God speaks to him in a dream that Sarai is another man's wife.

> But God came to Abimelech in a dream by night, and said to him, Behold, thou art but a dead man, for the woman which thou hast taken; for she is a man's wife.
>
> But Abimelech had not come near her: and he said, Lord, wilt thou slay also a righteous nation?

Said he not unto me, She is my sister? and she, even she herself said, He is my brother: in the integrity of my heart and innocency of my hands have I done this.

And God said unto him in a dream, Yea, I know that thou didst this in the integrity of thy heart; for I also withheld thee from sinning against me: therefore suffered I thee not to touch her.

Now therefore restore the man his wife; for he is a prophet, and he shall pray for thee, and thou shalt live: and if thou restore her not, know thou that thou shalt surely die, thou, and all that are thine.

GENESIS 20:3-7

Abimelech calls Abram to his house and says, "How dare you! You trying to get me killed? Do you understand God spoke to me and had me stand up for your wife because you wouldn't?" Abram did not do his job as a husband, so God had to call on an unbeliever to step in and protect Sarai! That just shows you wives the lengths God will go to in order to keep you safe even when your own husbands are carried away with fear and don't do the right thing.

This account of Abram illustrates the disaster that happens when believers try to get someone else to fight the battle God has called them to fight.

7. Fear is forgivable. In 1 John 1:7 the Bible tells us, "But if we walk in the light, as he is in the light, we have fellowship one with another, and the blood of Jesus Christ his Son cleanseth us from all sin." When you look at what Abram did to Sarai—telling everyone she was his sister and even letting the king take her into his harem in order to save his own skin— you wonder how God could have picked such a despicable character as His prophet (see Gen. 20:7). First John 1:7 tells us how: Abram messed up, but he still continued to walk with God, so God forgave him and blessed him and used him.

This is important for you to know as a child of God. God sees you as a perfect human being because He sees you through the blood of Jesus, just like He saw Abram. Don't attempt to criminalize Abram. He was walking with God. Abram is the father of our faith and our example. He made some pretty bad mistakes, but he repented and continued to walk with God, and God used him in a mighty way. If we walk in the light with God and have fellowship with Him, the blood of Jesus cleanses us from ALL sin. If we mess up, we veer off the path, or turn away from God for a moment and sin, all we have to do is get back in fellowship with God and He will forgive us and cleanse us.

When you walk in the light of what you understand and what you know, God doesn't judge you for the things that you don't understand and know. When you first came to Jesus you could sit there sucking beers, smoking pot, and having fellowship with Jesus and He didn't run away. But the moment you came to the understanding that smoking pot displeases God, guilt showed up and you knew you were supposed to stop.

Abram was a man who walked with God and loved his wife, but his fear for his own life overcame his love for God and his wife. Even when he sinned, however, God came into the picture and not only saved them both but blessed them in the process. Fear is the absence of faith, and it is impossible to please God without faith (see Heb. 11:6), but fear is also forgivable.

8. **Fear tries to make you control others.** The best example of this is found in John, chapter 21. This is after Jesus' resurrection and before He ascended into heaven. He is walking on the beach talking to Peter.

> *So when they had dined, Jesus saith to Simon Peter, Simon, son of Jonas, lovest thou me more than these? He saith unto him, Yea, Lord; thou knowest that I love thee. He saith unto him, Feed my lambs.*
>
> *He saith to him again the second time, Simon, son of Jonas, lovest thou me? He saith unto him, Yea, Lord; thou knowest that I love thee. He saith unto him, Feed my sheep.*

He saith unto him the third time, Simon, son of Jonas, lovest thou me? Peter was grieved because he said unto him the third time, Lovest thou me? And he said unto him, Lord, thou knowest all things; thou knowest that I love thee. Jesus saith unto him, Feed my sheep.

Verily, verily, I say unto thee, When thou wast young, thou girdedst thyself, and walkedst whither thou wouldest: but when thou shalt be old, thou shalt stretch forth thy hands, and another shall gird thee, and carry thee whither thou wouldest not.

This spake he, signifying by what death he should glorify God. And when he had spoken this, he saith unto him, Follow me.

Then Peter, turning about, seeth the disciple whom Jesus loved following; which also leaned on his breast at supper, and said, Lord, which is he that betrayeth thee?

Peter seeing him saith to Jesus, Lord, and what shall this man do?

Jesus saith unto him, If I will that he tarry till I come, what is that to thee? follow thou me.

JOHN 21:15-22

Jesus restores Peter to Himself and his walk with God, then tells him about the rest of his life and ministry, as well as how he will die for Him. Just then Peter looks aside and sees John. Fear grabs hold of Peter and he asks Jesus what is going to happen to John, but Jesus tells Peter that it is none of his business! He tells Peter not to worry about what's going on in the life of somebody else. Peter's job is to do what He has called him to do.

Worry and fear will cause you to get into someone else's life when you should be minding your own life. In Matthew, chapter 7, Jesus gives us a thorough explanation of how this works.

Judge not, that ye be not judged.

For with what judgment ye judge, ye shall be judged: and with what measure ye mete, it shall be measured to you again.

And why beholdest thou the mote that is in thy brother's eye, but considerest not the beam that is in thine own eye?

Or how wilt thou say to thy brother, Let me pull out the mote out of thine eye; and, behold, a beam is in thine own eye?

Thou hypocrite, first cast out the beam out of thine own eye; and then shalt thou see clearly to cast out the mote out of thy brother's eye.

MATTHEW 7:1-5

This passage of Scripture tells me that the moment I pass judgment on you I actually condemn myself because I am doing the very same thing. And the result is that I'm so consumed with getting you straight and controlling your life— to make me feel better—that I have no time or mental capacity to do what God called me to do.

Worry and fear try to make you control others, convincing you that you have to control every situation to feel safe and secure. Why? You have no faith in God to keep you safe and secure, to see that whatever happens to you becomes a blessing in your life.

When you are fearful, you try to control everyone; but when you have faith in God, you can love everyone and trust God to lead them and guide them. Then you are free and can do what God called you to do.

9. Faith is the mastery of fear, not the absence of fear. Fear must be mastered because you are always going to have to deal with it in this life. You'll never completely get rid of it. To master fear, you must establish a foundation on the rock of God's Word.

And why call ye me, Lord, Lord, and do not the things which I say?

Whosoever cometh to me, and heareth my sayings, and doeth them, I will show you to whom he is like:

He is like a man which built an house, and digged deep, and laid the foundation on a rock: and when the flood arose, the stream beat

196

vehemently upon that house, and could not shake it: for it was founded upon a rock.

But he that heareth, and doeth not, is like a man that without a foundation built an house upon the earth; against which the stream did beat vehemently, and immediately it fell; and the ruin of that house was great.

LUKE 6:46-49

In Luke, chapter 6, Jesus asked His disciples why they called Him Lord but didn't obey His Word. He said that only when you hear His Word and live His Word will you stay safe and overcome whatever disaster or attack the enemy throws at you. So you must establish the truth in your heart—that's your foundation. And that foundation is the platform on which you master any worry, fear, or terror that comes your way. Many Scriptures tell us the same thing.

He shall not be afraid of evil tidings: his heart is fixed, trusting in the LORD.

PSALM 112:7

10. Resist everything that comes against the truth. There is a principle that any statement that goes unchallenged is considered fact. Any unchallenged statement is automatically established as truth. When someone comes up to me and goes on and on about their opinion, and their opinion is contrary to the Word of God, I must stop their little filibuster and set the record straight by speaking the truth. If I don't do that, if I never say anything, they will think that what they're saying is right and that I agreed with them.

James 4:7 tells us, "Submit yourselves therefore to God. Resist the devil, and he will flee from you." We must remember to resist anything that comes against the truth. Resisting the devil is often a hard thing for believers to learn. When the devil comes around, we almost always say, "Why is the devil picking on me? There's got to be something wrong with God. There's got to be something wrong with my church. There's got to be something wrong with what I've been taught." We resist everything but the devil! How does that happen?

When we become God's children we think our lives will now be perfect. And if we think our lives should be perfect then we fall into pride. Then things get really bad because pride comes before destruction (see Prov. 16:18), and all the devil has to do is come in with a temptation or trial to bring us down. But the Bible says to humble ourselves before God so we will have the courage and wisdom to resist the devil. And when we resist the devil in God's strength and understanding, he will always flee from us.

When you resist everything that comes against the truth, you are resisting the lies of the devil and standing in the truth. And when you stand in truth, terror cannot prevail in your life.

11. Cast down vain reasoning. We know that the Bible says that God wants to sit and talk with us. He says in Isaiah 1:18, "Come now, and let us reason together, saith the LORD." When we meditate on God's Word, the Holy Spirit reveals to us God's way of thinking, His logic, and His reasoning. Then we can begin to think and speak and act like God.

There is another kind of human reasoning that reduces God's logic and reasoning to the point where the truth is cancelled out and we believe a lie. That is the kind of reasoning that is vain, empty, and devilish; and we need to cast it down and kick it out of our lives.

> *For though we walk in the flesh, we do not war after the flesh:*
> *(For the weapons of our warfare are not carnal, but mighty*
> *through God to the pulling down of strong holds;)*

Casting down imaginations, and every high thing that exalteth itself against the knowledge of God, and bringing into captivity every thought to the obedience of Christ.

2 CORINTHIANS 10:3-5

In the *New International Version* it says "casting down reasonings." We are to cast down the reasonings that try to call God's Word a lie. If you are going to walk free from terror, you must get rid of devilish reasoning. The devil will attempt to get you into a thought process or progression of thoughts that will lead you to the conclusion that the Word of God cannot be trusted and is simply not true. Sometimes you will "figure out" that the Word is just not true for you. You are the exception the Word of God just doesn't work for. You will find all kinds of "reasons" why the Word doesn't work for you.

To overcome terror and fear in your life, you must cast these false reasonings down, refuse to think along those lines, and bring your mind back to what the Word of God says. Then you have that solid foundation to stand on and are full of faith.

12. Hold on! If I'm going to beat fear in my life, all I need to do is hold on because Jesus has already defeated every enemy of my soul. You know this is a game of longevity. The one who wins is simply the last man standing. So I just don't quit. I tell my congregation that weebles wobble but they don't fall down. You might see me wobbling, on one foot, and my car on two wheels, but I'm in motion and I'm not stopping until I reach the destination God has ordained for me to reach.

I might be messed up. My thinking might be screwed up. I might not have my act together at the moment. But you can put your money down on the fact that I'm not quitting. Hebrews 10:23 commands us to hold on to our confession of faith without wavering. We are literally to tie ourselves to our confession of faith in God and His Word. The *New Living Trans-*

lation says, "Without wavering, let us hold tightly to the hope we say we have, for God can be trusted to keep his promise."

> *Do not throw away this confident trust in the Lord, no matter what happens. Remember the great reward it brings you!*
>
> *Patient endurance is what you need now, so you will continue to do God's will. Then you will receive all that he has promised.*
>
> *For in just a little while, the Coming One will come and not delay.*
>
> *And a righteous person will live by faith. But I will have no pleasure in anyone who turns away."*
>
> *But we are not like those who turn their backs on God and seal their fate. We have faith that assures our salvation.*
>
> HEBREWS 10:35-39 NLT

Hold on! God's greatest disappointment is that man would give up just before freedom is obtained and terror overcome.

THE STAKES ARE HIGH

We've been given stewardship of our nation. What are we passing to our children? What are we giving to them? If we ignore terrorism and just have a party, someone is eventually going to have to pay the check.

When I was about twelve, we went to a restaurant to eat but no one could pay for the meals we ordered. So we all got up and went toward the bathrooms and then ran out of the restaurant. We thought we had really gotten away with something, but someone ended up paying our bill.

That's why it is so important for believers to live by faith and overcome fear in our time. Whatever we do, whatever truth we walk in, we will pass that to the next generation. I believe that for the last thirty years, Satan's kingdom has been able to lull the church in America to sleep, rendering us inactive and ineffective concerning the things that we believed. From the passing of pro-abortion legislation to taking prayer out of and putting sex education in public schools, we have allowed the enemy to destroy and cripple the next generation.

The Bible gives us clear instructions about how we are to make the path straight for generations to come.

> *Finally, my brethren, be strong in the Lord, and in the power of his might.*
>
> *Put on the whole armour of God, that ye may be able to stand against the wiles of the devil.*
>
> *For we wrestle not against flesh and blood, but against principalities, against powers, against the rulers of the darkness of this world, against spiritual wickedness in high places.*
>
> *Wherefore take unto you the whole armour of God, that ye may be able to withstand in the evil day, and having done all, to stand.*
>
> EPHESIANS 6:10-13

We are to be strong in God, to trust in His armor, and to stand against the strategies and tricks of the devil. Why? Because if we do not fight and defeat the real terrorists, who are behind every terrorist act in the earthly realm, then who will? No one else has authority of them. We must wield the authority we have in Jesus' name to defeat evil rulers and authorities of the spirit realm, powers of darkness and wicked spirits that cause every evil situation in our world. Only the armor of God and the strength of the Lord can overcome anxiety and terror in this earth.

If we walk in terror, the next generation will be subject to terror. But if we walk in faith and defeat anxiety and terror in our lives, the next generation will know how to do the same to preserve our nation and bring God's peace to a troubled and lost world.

1 7

God Delivers Us From Worry

After this manner therefore pray ye: Our Father which art in heaven, Hallowed be thy name.

Thy kingdom come. Thy will be done in earth, as it is in heaven.

Give us this day our daily bread.

And forgive us our debts, as we forgive our debtors.

And lead us not into temptation, but deliver us from evil: For thine is the kingdom, and the power, and the glory, for ever. Amen.

MATTHEW 6:9-13

The entire Bible is filled with Scriptures that talk about how God is our deliverer. He delivers us from eternal damnation and wrath through the blood of Jesus; and He delivers us from the devil, the world, and the flesh while we are here on earth. That's why Jesus instructed us to pray that God would deliver us from evil in Matthew 6:13 above.

By now in this book, I hope you are recognizing how evil worry can be. Jesus knew that everywhere we would turn, Satan would try to upset us, to make us suspicious of everyone and everything, and to get us to worry about everything that concerns us. He wants to kill anything that has any life in it and to destroy the future God has planned for us. But we can rejoice when we pray, "God, deliver us from evil," because He has a plan to do just that.

DELIVERANCE IS BIBLICAL

God delivers us so that we can walk through this life without the shackles of worry about eternity or during our lifetime on earth. He takes the shackles off our feet and sets us free from all fear of the future. But He can't take the shackles off until we first admit what those shackles of fear are. A lot of times, we don't know what worries are encumbering us and wearing us down. But sometimes when we do discover that we are worried out of our minds about something, we are too proud or scared to admit it and ask for deliverance from it.

What does the word "deliverance" mean?

> 1. a setting free; rescue or release 2. The fact or state of being freed 3. an opinion, judgment, etc. formally or publicly expressed.[1]

You could say deliverance means to be set free from restraint, captivity, oppression, and to be rescued from danger. It can also mean to be acquitted from guilt (as a jury would acquit or declare not guilty someone accused of a crime). By the blood of Jesus we are acquitted from our sin and set free from all guilt and shame. God delivers us from a tremendous amount of worry and fear right there! The blood of Jesus delivers us from all worry and fear pertaining to this life as well as eternal life.

God delivers us in a multitude of ways, some of them highly creative and others very simple. But the important thing is that we get delivered. And I can tell you one thing from experience, whether He delivers you in a second when someone prays for you or whether He delivers you through a process, He always delivers you by His Word and the power of His Spirit. Then, to stay free, you must continue in His Word and communion with His Spirit.

Not only does God deliver us in a variety of ways, but also He delivers us from a lot of different things—all of them involve worry. We worry about dangerous situations. We worry about getting sick. We worry about being overcome by our enemies. We worry about becoming worried to the point of being dominated by fear instead of faith. We worry about dying. And we worry about committing sin. None of these things are too hard for God. He can deliver us from worrying about all of them.

DELIVERANCE FROM DANGER

In 1 Samuel 17:37, David went before Saul and said, "I killed a lion and a bear when they tried to kill my sheep, and this Philistine will be no different." Saul recognized the courage of the Lord in David and told him to go and fight Goliath. But why did David have the confidence and courage to fight a giant that all the stronger, more skilled warriors were afraid to face? David understood and had experienced God's deliverance from danger. He knew God would protect him and fight for him. *David was not worried.*

Being delivered out of the mouth of a lion is not something God did only for David or Old Testament believers.

> *Notwithstanding the Lord stood with me, and strengthened me; that by me the preaching might be fully known, and that all the Gentiles might hear: and I was delivered out of the mouth of the lion.*
>
> *And the Lord shall deliver me from every evil work, and will preserve me unto his heavenly kingdom: to whom be glory for ever and ever. Amen.*
>
> 2 TIMOTHY 4:17,18

The apostle Paul was speaking of how God delivered him, first from the lion. Personally, I believe he was referring to the roaring lion who seeks whom he may devour, Satan. He roars and makes a lot of noise to try to worry us and frighten us. He does this to keep us from living in the peace God has given us and doing what He's called us to do. But in these verses Paul says that Jesus stood with him, strengthened him, and delivered him from the lion. He delivered Paul from danger, and He will deliver you from danger, too. *You do not need to be worried!*

DELIVERANCE FROM SICKNESS

The blood of Jesus delivers us from sickness and disease. In Matthew 8:17 Jesus said that He came to fulfill Isaiah's prophecy: "Himself took our infirmities, and bare our sicknesses." Other Scriptures confirm the fact that our God is a healing God.

> *Bless the LORD, O my soul: and all that is within me, bless his holy name.*
>
> *Bless the LORD, O my soul, and forget not all his benefits:*
>
> *Who forgiveth all thine iniquities; who healeth all thy diseases.*
>
> PSALM 103:1-3

Jesus took your infirmities and bore your sicknesses. He forgives all your iniquities and heals all your diseases. So when you start getting sick, you don't have to worry because God delivers you from all sickness and disease. Just stand in faith in God and His Word and you will be healed. You can also call for the elders of your church to pray for you.

> *Is any sick among you? let him call for the elders of the church; and let them pray over him, anointing him with oil in the name of the Lord:*
>
> *And the prayer of faith shall save the sick, and the Lord shall raise him up.*
>
> JAMES 5:14

Old Testament and New Testament believers are delivered from sickness by the Lord. He raises us up when we anoint with oil and pray the prayer of faith.

DELIVERANCE FROM TROUBLE

No matter what comes our way—and trouble will come!—the Bible tells us that God is there to deliver us. Because we are His children and are righteous through the blood of Jesus Christ, He sees to it that we are delivered from all kinds of trouble in our lives.

> *The righteous cry, and the LORD heareth, and delivereth them out of all their troubles.*
> *Many are the afflictions of the righteous: but the LORD delivereth him out of them all.*
>
> PSALM 34:17,19

God said He's going to deliver you out of all your troubles! He's going to deliver you from every affliction. So you don't have to be worried when trouble comes your way.

DELIVERANCE FROM ENEMIES

Daniel was in the lions' den because his contemporaries were jealous of him. They were offended over the fact that he was a man of excellence, had great favor with the king, and they couldn't measure up. So they laid a trap for him. But Daniel went into that lions' den trusting God to deliver him. He didn't seem at all worried!

> *Then the king commanded, and they brought Daniel, and cast him into the den of lions. Now the king spake and said unto Daniel,* **Thy God whom thou servest continually, he will deliver thee.**
>
> DANIEL 6:16 (EMPHASIS MINE)

This is a very interesting verse of Scripture because both Daniel *and* the king had faith for God to deliver Daniel from his enemies.

> *And a stone was brought, and laid upon the mouth of the den; and the king sealed it with his own signet, and with the signet of his lords; that the purpose might not be changed concerning Daniel.*
>
> DANIEL 6:17

The purpose that the king was so careful to carry out was that Daniel be executed. His enemies had outwitted the king, who signed Daniel's execution without realizing it. Now the king is bound by his own law to carry it out. Let's read how God delivered Daniel.

> *Then the king went to his palace, and passed the night fasting: neither were instruments of music brought before him: and his sleep went from him.*
>
> *Then the king arose very early in the morning, and went in haste unto the den of lions.*
>
> *And when he came to the den, he cried with a lamentable voice unto Daniel: and the king spake and said to Daniel, O Daniel, servant of the living God, is thy God, whom thou servest continually, able to deliver thee from the lions?*
>
> *Then said Daniel unto the king, O king, live for ever.*
>
> **My God hath sent his angel, and hath shut the lions' mouths, that they have not hurt me:** *forasmuch as before him innocency was found in me; and also before thee, O king, have I done no hurt.*
>
> *Then was the king exceeding glad for him, and commanded that they should take Daniel up out of the den. So Daniel was taken up out of the den, and no manner of hurt was found upon him, because* **he believed in his God.**
>
> DANIEL 6:18-23 (EMPHASIS MINE)

Daniel was not hurt because "he believed in his God." When you believe in your God, you aren't worried. Do you see that? And the Bible says that when you believe in God, He will deliver you from your enemies.

In Luke the Bible tells us about the birth of John the Baptist. Zacharias, John's father, was filled with the Holy Spirit and prophesied of Jesus:

> *Blessed be the Lord God of Israel; for he hath visited and redeemed his people,*
>
> *And hath raised up an horn of salvation for us in the house of his servant David;*
>
> *As he spake by the mouth of his holy prophets, which have been since the world began:*
>
> **That we should be saved from our enemies, and from the hand of all that hate us.**
>
> LUKE 1:68-71 (EMPHASIS MINE)

The horn (or ruler) of salvation who was descended from David was Jesus. Why was Jesus being sent? "That we should be saved from our enemies." In 2 Thessalonians 3:2 says Jesus came, "that we may be delivered from unreasonable and wicked men." If you have ever spoken with an unreasonable or wicked person, you know how important this verse is! You don't need to worry, however, because God will always deliver you from them.

DELIVERANCE FROM FEAR

> *I sought the Lord, and he heard me, and delivered me from all my fears.*
>
> PSALM 34:4

This verse of Scripture paints a clear picture of what we are supposed to do the moment we become afraid of something.

We are to seek the Lord, and the Word of God then assures us that He will hear us and deliver us from that fear.

> *For God hath not given us the spirit of fear; but of power, and of love, and of a sound mind.*
>
> 2 TIMOTHY 1:7

No fear. Power, love, and a sound mind. You don't have to walk around thinking that no one is backing you up, because you have the Creator of heaven and earth at your back! You don't have to be afraid that no one loves you, because your Father God loves you. And finally, you don't have to wonder if you have the brains to do what you're called to do, because you have the mind of Christ, and Jesus has the soundest mind of all human beings ever on the planet.

When you were born again, God didn't give you a new spirit that was subject to fear. He gave you a new spirit that was free from fear. When you think, speak, and act from your born-again spirit, the source of your power, love, and wisdom is the Holy Spirit. He lives in your spirit and is the source of the authority you walk in by the name of Jesus.

> *There is no fear in love; but perfect love casteth out fear.*
>
> 1 JOHN 4:18

The love of God casts out all fear. Having a sound mind means understanding that you aren't useless, valueless, hopeless, and powerless because God loves you. With God's love, you don't have to worry about being afraid.

DELIVERANCE FROM THE FEAR OF DEATH

The Bible tells us in Hebrews 2:14 that this was one of the main reasons Jesus came to earth, one of the main things He came to deliver us from. It says, "For as much then as the children are partakers of flesh and blood, he also himself likewise took part of the same that through death, he might destroy him that had the power of death, that is the devil." Then in verse 15, it says, "And deliver them who through their fear of death were all their lifetimes subject to bondage."

Have you ever been afraid you were going to die? Every man, woman, and child experiences the fear of death at one time or another. The reason for this is because fear of death is Satan's ace card. We are all going to die. Even the Bible says in Hebrews 9:27 that every one of us has a set time to die. Of course, should the rapture occur before believers die, they will not see death the way other people do. But if Jesus tarries, then you and I will face physical death. Satan knows this and tries to scare everybody with it. That's why God sent Jesus to deliver us from the fear of death.

Do you realize that a person who is afraid they're going to die is in bondage? Every day they think they're not going to make it. Every day they're wondering if this may be the last day. Every ache or pain convinces them that they have a terminal disease and their days are numbered. Every accident or catastrophe on the news chokes them with worry about their own future.

O death, where is thy sting? O grave, where is thy victory?

1 CORINTHIANS 15:55

If you have been in bondage through the fear of death, you need to meditate on these Scriptures and thank God for delivering you from that fear. Jesus destroyed the destroyer! So you don't have to worry about death any longer. Instead, you can thank God for His love, His power, and the mind of Christ He's given you. Rejoice that when it's your time to leave this planet, death will have no sting because you are going straight to heaven!

DELIVERANCE FROM SIN

God delivers me from myself! The person you know who sins the most is yourself. That person is not across the street; that person is in your own skin. Do you ever think about the fact that you know more sins about yourself than anyone else?

When I came to the realization that the person who sinned more than anybody else that I knew was me, I decided that I needed to go to work on that two-by-four that was stuck in my eye and leave other people alone with their little toothpicks in their eyes! Some of us have toothpick vision and others of us have plank vision.

Thank God, He delivers us from plank vision and all kinds of sins. Galatians 1:4 says Jesus "gave himself for our sins, that he might deliver us from this present evil world." And some of the most powerful pictures of Jesus delivering us from our sins are found in the book of Revelation.

> *And from Jesus Christ, who is the faithful witness, and the first begotten of the dead, and the prince of the kings of the earth. Unto him that loved us, and washed us from our sins in his own blood.*
>
> REVELATION 1:5

> *And I saw a strong angel proclaiming with a loud voice, Who is worthy to open the book, and to loose the seals thereof?*
>
> *And no man in heaven, nor in earth, neither under the earth, was able to open the book, neither to look thereon.*
>
> *And I wept much, because no man was found worthy to open and to read the book, neither to look thereon.*
>
> *And one of the elders saith unto me, Weep not: behold, the Lion of the tribe of Judah, the Root of David, hath prevailed to open the book, and to loose the seven seals thereof.*

And I beheld, and, lo, in the midst of the throne and of the four beasts, and in the midst of the elders, stood a Lamb as it had been slain, having seven horns and seven eyes, which are the seven Spirits of God sent forth into all the earth.

And he came and took the book out of the right hand of him that sat upon the throne.

And when he had taken the book, the four beasts and four and twenty elders fell down before the Lamb, having every one of them harps, and golden vials full of odours, which are the prayers of saints.

And they sung a new song, saying, Thou art worthy to take the book, and to open the seals thereof: for thou wast slain, and hast redeemed us to God by thy blood out of every kindred, and tongue, and people, and nation;

And hast made us unto our God kings and priests: and we shall reign on the earth.

REVELATION 5:2-10 (ITALICS MINE)

Jesus came to deliver you from your sins for eternity, and that includes right now. He not only delivers you from yourself, but also He delivers you from all of the things the world and the devil throw at you to try to get you to sin. The Holy Spirit and the Word of God live inside you to help you resist sin and walk in the righteousness of Christ.

You don't need to be worried about whether you're going to be able to serve God well because the Holy Spirit inside you will keep you straight, and the Bible tells you that if you do sin, you have an advocate with the Father, Jesus. Jesus Himself is going to plead your case when the devil comes to accuse you of sin. First John 1:9 tells us that when you do sin, all you have to do is confess it, and God forgives you—and cleanses you from any unrighteousness in your life. That's a very good deal!

God delivers us from our danger, illness, trouble, enemies, fear, fear of death, and sin. We don't have to run around worrying about all these things.

Thou art my hiding place; thou shalt preserve me from trouble;
thou shalt compass me about with songs of deliverance.

PSALM 32:7

1 8

Dealing With Stress

There are many vicious cycles we can fall into while we are here on planet earth. Personally, the one that I believe we all fight in our time today is the cycle of worry and stress. Stress causes worry, and worry causes stress. This vicious cycle is a fact of modern life because everything and everybody move so fast. From supersonic jets to cell phones, human beings are on the run.

Stress is something all people have to deal with. Most people are exposed to much higher levels of stress than they realize. Our brain cells talk to each other, and when a person is exposed to too much stress the communication in the brain begins to fail. You actually have three centers in your brain that communicate with each other. When you become overstressed, you have a communication breakdown, which then manifests in sleep disorders, sleep disturbance, aches and pains, a lack of energy, and being depressed without knowing why.

THE GOOD AND BAD OF OVERSTRESSED

Because stress is a fact of our lives and will most likely increase instead of decrease, we must learn how to deal with it. But first we need to understand it. Let me ask you a question. Which of these do you think causes stress?

- Getting a promotion on your job.

- Getting a flat tire.
- Having new furniture delivered.
- Your best friend and his wife coming to visit for a week.

The answer is: Every one of these things causes stress. Whether you enjoy an activity or not, stress is involved. People don't realize that stress doesn't have to come from a bad situation. It is simply over-using your body and soul. Overstress can happen simply because you have too much going on in your life. That's why many ministers suffer burnout. They are doing good things but neglecting their personal health and needs to the point where their minds and bodies just give out.

Stress is many different kinds of things to many different people. It's happy things. It's sad things. It's physical things. It's mental things. Many people carry enormous stress loads, and some don't even know it because they are having such a good time. They enjoy their jobs. They enjoy working out every morning. They enjoy running the kids to lessons and ball games. They enjoy three projects going at once. Some people even enjoy sitting for hours solving problems or creating something new. No matter how much fun they are having, however, there is still a level of stress on their minds and bodies.

As I began to take a look at this subject I saw that certain families handle stress differently than other families. It's genetic. Members of one family will blow up at the smallest amount of stress, while members of another family will stay focused without freaking out. You can't judge them because the ones who react immediately may be relieving the stress while the ones who stay focused and don't react may have a meltdown later on.

No matter how you behave or whether the stress comes from a positive event or a negative event, your body sees stress as stress. And it sees it as change. It understands it as change.

Interestingly enough, your mind is so sophisticated that even imagined change is stress. When your mind imagines that something is changing, your body reacts to that imagination. The Bible tells us the same thing in Proverbs 23:7, "For as he thinketh in his heart, so is he."

CAUSES OF STRESS

There are so many ways we can be stressed. There's emotional stress when arguments, disagreements, and conflicts arise. Any strain in a relationship is stressful. There's physical stress. Whether you get a cold, the flu, or you're dealing with a chronic runny nose, some kind of stress is going on. The physical problem is caused by overstress, and the body's process or method of healing often causes more stress.

There are a number of countries that understand that pushing yourself too hard can be stressful. We have to have a vacation when we get back from vacation! You hear people say things like, "I can hardly wait to go back to work because I can finally get some rest." Some people play so hard that they get overstressed from it.

What causes stress more than anything, remember, is change. Whenever you alter your schedule or try to establish a new habit, it is stressful. If you begin to stay up later than usual but continue to get up early for work, you're not getting the same amount of rest. This is stressful. By doing this over time you set yourself up for physical sickness. Without enough rest your immune system gets weaker and eventually your body will break down in some way.

The word *disease* is interesting if you hyphenate it: dis-ease. What this indicates is that sickness and illness mean you are not at ease. Worry and stress are the opposite of not being at ease. Although the body and mind must be exercised and used to stay healthy, overuse and overstress are the extreme that cause dis-ease.

JOY IN THE HOLY SPIRIT

After we are born again, we still live on planet earth and must deal with stress. What is our biblical example of how to handle stress and stop worrying?

> *For our gospel came not unto you in word only, but also in power, and in the Holy Ghost, and in much assurance; as ye know what manner of men we were among you for your sake.*
>
> *And ye became followers of us, and of the Lord, having received the word in much affliction, with joy of the Holy Ghost:*
>
> *So that ye were ensamples to all that believe in Macedonia and Achaia.*
>
> 1 THESSALONIANS 1:5-7 (EMPHASIS MINE)

The apostle Paul was writing to the Thessalonian church, where the believers' lives were in absolute shambles for the gospel's sake. They had lost their businesses, and many had lost loved ones. They lost their homes and were turned out into the street. Yet the joy of the Holy Spirit sustained them so much that Paul says they are examples, heroes of the faith, to all believers. Although great pressure was placed upon them, the joy of the Holy Spirit was evident even in the darkest days.

I don't know a lot of believers who handle stress well. Most are kicking and screaming at the slightest setback, obstacle, or challenge in their lives. I believe one of the problems is that over the last thirty or forty years we have talked a lot about prosperity and healing and not a lot about crucifying the flesh. We have produced a generation of believers who think the prosperity and healing message means that Christians don't have to endure affliction. Whenever they encounter any type of difficulty in their lives they simply rebuke the devil. They ought to be rebuking themselves and drawing on the joy of the Holy Ghost!

These Christians focus on getting the victory in whatever uncomfortable situation they find themselves. But they never allow the Holy Spirit to fill them with the same joy the Thessalonians had during their affliction. Why? Because the Thessalonians also crucified their flesh, put off the old man, and learned to have a good attitude no matter what was going on in their lives. They not only persevered in the affliction, but they grew up in God in the affliction.

How You Deal With Stress Matters

The truth is, just because you know you will ultimately have the victory in Christ, you cannot do whatever you want to do and act however you feel like acting while things are uncomfortable. In fact, you can stop your victory from coming if you continue to act according to the flesh and do not walk in the fruit of the Spirit. It causes more stress to act according to the flesh because we continue in anger, frustration, and worry. On the other hand, if we put to death the deeds of the flesh and walk in faith, we cancel out any anger, frustration, or worry that would arise.

As a pastor, I see all sorts of emotions with people every day. In one day I can do a funeral and deal with death and grief in the morning, meet with a troubled married couple and deal with anger and violence in the afternoon, and do a wedding and deal with ecstatic love and joy in the evening. Going through all those emotions in one day is like riding an emotional roller coaster. There are times when I really want to feel sorry for myself!

How do I deal with this stress? Jesus gave me the answer when He said that the whole law is summed up in two commandments: loving God with all your heart, soul, mind, and strength; and loving your neighbor as yourself. (See Matt. 22:37-40.) First, I have to stick close to God and His Word and love Him more than my own life. I have to remember that He loves me, and He's called me to do what I do, so He's going to empower me to do it. I remind myself that I can do all things through Christ who strengthens me; and in my weakness, His strength comes in and gives me the mental, emotional, and physical ability to do what He's called me to do. (See Phil. 4:13 and 2 Cor. 12:10.) When I live and move and have my being in God and His Word, I have the joy of the Lord which is my strength. (See Acts 17:28 and Neh. 8:10.) This is the joy that the Thessalonians experienced in their affliction. They loved God more than their own lives.

The second part of the two great commandments is loving your neighbor as you love yourself. One day I realized that there is no person that ever walks through the doors of our church who is an island unto themselves. Every person is linked to other people. There is a mathematical principle that every person is only four people away from touching every person on the entire earth. If this is true, then your stress touches the person on the other side of the building. Your attitude will affect the person at the end of your row.

There is a lie in the church that comes from the world, and that is that you can sin and it won't affect anyone but you. You can be a ball of worry, and no one around you will be affected. But in 1 Corinthians 12:12-26 the Bible talks about the body of Christ as being members one of another, that we have need of one another, that we are connected in the Spirit, that when one member suffers we all suffer, and when one member rejoices we all rejoice. That says to me that what I do affects the entire body of Christ in the same way my whole body feels it when I stub my toe, sing a song, smell a skunk, or eat an orange.

The reason handling stress well matters is because it affects everyone around you. The way a believer deals with a stressful situation can change the lives—for better or worse—of all the people with whom that believer is connected.

LIVING WISELY

My desire is that every believer be the best they can be in Christ and do all that God has called them to do. I care for the people of God and want them to be successful and flourish in the things of God. To do that, we must have wisdom in living our lives. Faith does not mean we can live any way we please and expect God to fulfill His promises and bless us. Yes, He gives us grace and mercy at times, but we are responsible to meet the conditions of His promises and obey His Word and Spirit.

The Bible has a lot to say about how we are to live our daily lives, and most of it has to do with discipline of the flesh. Here are three things that have helped me to minimize the cycle of worry and stress.

1. Consistency. Proverbs 11:1 says, "A false balance is abomination to the Lord, but a just weight is His delight." Consistency brings balance into your life. Sometimes you have to give up short-term gratification for long-term blessing. For example, consistent giving may mean giving up something today, but it will mean continual and greater financial blessings down the road. As I discipline myself to give consistently, I am giving up a pleasure for the moment for the long-term life of blessings. If I spend my offering on myself today, I will enjoy it today; but if I give my offering as a seed in God's kingdom, I will enjoy it for many days to come as it brings a harvest in my life. In the long run I will have less stress—and far less worry—because I give consistently.

Another area where consistency pays off is in the daily reading and study of the Bible with prayer. Personally, I don't know how you can separate the two. The Holy Spirit teaches us and often leads us and guides us through God's Word, and while we are reading and studying, prayer and communion with God just come naturally. When you neglect this special, private time with the Lord, over time you will dry up spiritually. Remember "Give us day by day our daily bread" (Luke 11:3) and "man shall not live by bread alone, but by every word of God" (Luke 4:4)? If we do not feed our soul and spirit God's Word every day, we will waste away spiritually. On the other hand, when we feast on the Word and pray every day, over time we will see great peace, wisdom, strength, and success come into our lives.

2. Wisdom in taking responsibility. We have talked about this before. Never allow others to transfer their responsibilities to you. Don't take on the responsibility that belongs to somebody else. In my church we have mothers whose young teenage daughters have had babies out-of-wedlock. A mother naturally wants to help, and she loves her daughter and grandchild. But she makes a big mistake if she steps in and becomes that baby's mother instead of allowing her daughter to take responsibility for her child. When she offers to take care of the baby and buy for the baby, she is actually hindering her daughter from becoming the mother she's supposed to be. Why? Because she assumed her daughter's responsibility.

In 1 Thessalonians 4:11 the Bible tells us to "do your own business." Do you realize that when you begin to take the responsibilities of someone else you are not doing what you've been told to do? Think about it. If you are taking on the responsibilities of other people, then you are not doing what God has called you to do. And that causes stress and worry that God can't help you with because you are not obeying Him. So we must never take on responsibilities that God hasn't given us.

3. Cast all your cares on God. When I'm dealing with my congregation and all of their problems and joys—all which cause stress or worry—I have to cast all my cares on God and remind myself that He cares for me. First Peter 5:6 says, "Humble yourselves therefore under the mighty hand of God, that he may exalt you in due time: Casting all your care upon him; for he careth for you." I have to humble myself under God's mighty hand and trust that He will exalt me in due time. But I'm not going to be exalted until I've rolled all my cares on Him.

I have had to learn that I cannot take responsibility for what's going on in another person's life. I can't change the things that are happening with other people, but I CAN pray and turn it over to God. I can't change it, but I can put it under God's delivering hand. I know that I will be exalted when I roll my cares on God. Sometimes I pray, "Lord, I don't know how Moses did it. I don't know how You did it, Jesus."

I always have to remind myself that it's God's church, not my church. I'm just a steward. I'm not the owner. He's the only one who can tell me what is the best course to take or the best decision to make. My job is to obey Him and cast all my care on Him.

Have you learned to roll your cares on God? Have you recognized the things that are other people's responsibilities, that you need to leave with them and not take on yourself? And are you consistent in your life? Do you keep a daily routine of prayer and Bible study? Do you get enough rest? All these things help us to effectively deal with stress and avoid worry.

1 9

God's Answer to Fear's Domination

If we continue to worry, then there is only one place we are going to end up: dominated by fear. How does that happen? Worrying is just a form of fear, but it doesn't seem to be as serious as fear. So we just keep worrying without really taking notice of the fact that we are worrying more and more. When we don't deal with worrying about something, that worry will grow into a full-blown, debilitating fear that will dominate us in everything we do.

Fear can also come unexpectedly. Something that has never happened to you occurs—you see something on television that is horrifying, someone tells you a story that paints a terrible picture in your mind, or a single thought can come out of nowhere and pierce you like a knife—then fear swings its scepter into your life. It will attack anytime it gets an opening. Today it must be fairly easy because people are afraid of everything. They're afraid to live; they're afraid to die. They're afraid to succeed; they're afraid to fail. They're afraid to stay where they are; they're afraid to try something different. They are just plain afraid.

Fear is a cruel master. It is such a cruel master that it will begin to control your life in evil ways. It will control your countenance, turning your bright and hopeful face into a dark frown. It will control the things you do, often driving you to do things that you should not do. Fear will rule over you in such a way that it will trap you in a corner, and it will not be satisfied until it absolutely destroys everything that God created you to be and do.

FEAR AND FAITH

Have you ever been so afraid that you didn't know what to do? That's being dominated by fear. You just pace the floor or sit staring into space—going nowhere. What you need to remember at times like these is that fear is faith in what the devil does instead of what God is doing. Fear is faith in the devil's ability to destroy your life instead of faith in God to preserve and provide for your life.

You will either magnify the devil and his power or you will magnify God and His power. Fear is faith in the wrong thing. Fear is believing something will go wrong. And when it does go wrong, it'll probably go wrong with you. You are convinced that you are doomed.

Fear speaks to you. It tells you that you don't want to ride in planes. It tells you that you can't go to certain places or be with certain people. It tells you that food is your enemy and you can't eat or you will be fat. It tells you that you must dress a certain way or people will not like you. It tells you that you must never tell anyone what is bothering you or people will reject you and look down on you.

As a result of listening to fear, you're afraid of losing your spouse or family. You're afraid of losing your job or business. You're afraid of getting old and sick and having no one to take care of you. You're afraid of not having enough money. You're afraid your kids are going to grow up and become drug addicts and criminals. You're afraid of committing yourself to someone in marriage because either you will become miserable or they will become miserable.

Fear has no face, but it has a voice. In Psalm 23, David referred to it as the "shadow of death." "Yea, though I walk through the valley of the shadow of death, I will fear no evil." Fear is a shadow. It is something we *think* is there, but we can't see it. We feel it, we sense it, and it's causing all kinds of fearful thoughts, but we can't see it.

In Luke 21:26 Jesus said that men's hearts would fail because of fear over things to come. In other words, they are not sure what is coming, but they are afraid of what might be coming. Instead of planning for victory, they plan for catastrophe and defeat. Fear causes people to actually plan for failure.

Faith in God, on the other hand, causes you to plan wisely and trust God for the rest. But most people will say things like, "I'll tell you what. As soon as I go down and make reservations for my vacation, I'll probably lose my job." Their whole idea of life is only what the devil is doing, not what God is doing. As a result, they expect one problem after another instead of one blessing after another.

Why do we spend time thinking about what's not? Why do we spend time thinking about something that we're not sure about? Why do we spend time thinking about things that just might happen? We spend *hours* there and cultivate fear when we could be spending hours with God's Word and the Holy Spirit cultivating faith. I think one of the reasons Christians fall into this is because they have not been taught about fiery trials.

THINK IT NOT STRANGE

The Christian life comes with trials and tribulations. The difference is in how we handle them. The Bible says in 1 Peter 4:12, "Beloved, think it not strange concerning the fiery trial which is to try you, as though some strange thing happened unto you." You are a child of God. Therefore, you should not think it a wild coincidence that the devil, his demons, the world system, and your flesh are going to do anything they can do to immobilize you with fear. Don't be surprised when you encounter a "fiery trial."

The next verse, 1 Peter 4:13, tells you why. "But rejoice, inasmuch as ye are partakers of Christ's sufferings; that, when his glory shall be revealed, ye may be glad also with exceeding joy." Whatever we encounter is designed to reveal the glory of God to us and through us. How we handle trials is one of the marks of believers; it is what makes us so different from unbelievers. And fear is a fiery trial that we can get through and overcome to the glory of God.

Remember, fear *is* a person. Fear has a personality. Fear has a voice, and it loves to take on *your* voice. It loves to make you think that those horrifying thoughts are your thoughts. That's *your* mind thinking, and you begin to act on those negative thoughts rather than the Word of God. When we let fear dominate our thinking, it begins to dominate our behavior and actions.

This is how it works. We have a worrisome thought, and we don't stop to recognize if it was our thought or a demonic thought. We just accept it as our thought. Because it is a worrisome thought, we then think that if we just stay quiet and don't make a lot of waves in this world, then nothing will happen. If we just leave well enough alone, shove that thought in the closet, and shut the door, everything's going to be just fine. We relax and hope it'll go away forever.

We do this year after year and then one day, we're driving down the road and the closet door flies open. Years of terrible thoughts come flying out and that's all we can think about. We are completely dominated by that fear and are wondering how on earth we got in this condition.

This happened to me just before I came into relationship with the Lord Jesus Christ, back in 1974. I was riding home from work, and I thought I had the world by the tail. But a fearful thought came into my mind. When I tried to push it away, it just came back stronger and every subconscious fear I had shoved away through the years became conscious.

From that moment on fear spoke to me every day. I couldn't eat. I couldn't sleep. I would work out and run in the evenings to get exhausted enough to sleep a few hours. Linda would wake up in the middle of the night and find me pacing the floor. I told her, "I'm just absolutely ravaged with fear!"

She would ask, "What are you afraid of?"

I would say, "I don't know. I'm just afraid. I'm so afraid I don't know what to do." Fear overtaking me; fear dominating me; fear speaking to me; fear not letting me go. Fear was a person that was controlling me. And I was afraid of everything.

> *The wicked is snared by the transgression of his lips: but the just shall come out of trouble.*
>
> *A man shall be satisfied with good by the fruit of his mouth: and the recompense of a man's hands shall be rendered unto him.*
>
> PROVERBS 12:13,14

When I came into relationship with Jesus and began studying the Word of God, I began to see that I had talked myself into my condition. I talked myself into being dominated by fear. First, I didn't deal with each worry as it came along in my life. I shoved them into the closet and all those worries didn't just stay there. They grew in power. And how did they do that? I added fuel to the fire of fear by speaking it out again and again.

"Well, I'm afraid you're right. I'm afraid that's true. I'm afraid that's going to happen. I'm afraid she's going to do that. I'm afraid I'm stuck. I'm afraid. I'm afraid. I'm afraid." Until one day, all of a sudden, my failure to deal with all those worries through the years brought forth the fruit of my lips. Everything I had ever said I was afraid of attacked me.

THE FEAR OF GOD

In Proverbs 1:7, the Bible tells us that the fear of God is the beginning of wisdom. So what is the difference between the fear of God and the ungodly fear that debilitates you? Ungodly fear is basically everything the devil wants to do to you so that you can't even think straight. He wants you to make decisions based on fear instead of faith in God. But the fear of God is a deep reverence that God is the almighty, holy Creator and you are His creation. As His child, you acknowledge who He is to you in every thought, word, and deed. Fearing God shuts the devil out.

When you fear God, you won't fear anything else because He's your whole world and focus. There's no room for any ungodly fear. That person called fear, whether it is in the form of a thought or a demon, can have no place in your life because you're too busy reverencing, serving, and loving God.

When you have the fear of the Lord is when you begin to learn how to make it in life. You do not fear what may happen or what did happen because it's all in His hands. You do not fear anyone else because there's no one else in life that you fear! It doesn't really matter what the doctor says because the last word comes from God's Word. It doesn't really matter what the lawyer says because the bottom line is what the Holy Spirit is telling you. It doesn't really matter what your spouse says because you can love them unconditionally through Him. It doesn't really matter what your boss says because the Bible tells you that He is your king and master. You are no longer operating on a multitude of fears. You are now operating on one fear: the fear of the Lord.

Living in the fear of the Lord is wisdom because in every issue of your life you want to know what He says about it. Fear can no longer talk your ear off, corner you, and paralyze you. You don't have time to listen to fear because you are too busy listening to the Lord.

If you don't fear God, you will be afraid of and intimidated by everything and everyone else. But fearing God puts you in a position of spiritual freedom, because in your mind and heart He is greater than anyone or anything in this life. Your fear of Him—deep reverence for who He is, what He says in His Word, and how He operates—crushes any other fear.

FEAR OF MAN

Some people are so afraid of what others think and say about them—or what they might do to them—that they calculate their every move to please them. Some people fear man so much that they even fear themselves! They're afraid of what they might say or do.

The fear of man brings a snare: but whosoever puts his trust in the LORD shall be kept safe.

PROVERBS 29:25

In the fear of man we go through a number of stages. We're afraid of what people think of us. We're afraid of what they don't think of us. We're afraid that they may judge us. We're afraid that they may not like us. When we fear men instead of God, we respect what other people think of us more than we respect what God thinks of us.

For example, if you fear God, how will that affect your relationship with your boss?

Servants, be obedient to them that are your masters according to the flesh, with fear and trembling, in singleness of your heart, as unto Christ;

Not with eyeservice, as menpleasers; but as the servants of Christ, doing the will of God from the heart;

With good will doing service, as to the Lord, and not to men:

Knowing that whatsoever good thing any man doeth, the same shall he receive of the Lord, whether he be bond or free.

EPHESIANS 6:5-8

The Bible says that we should serve others as though we were serving the Lord, then we can expect a good reward—but our reward comes from Him. He may bring the reward through our boss, but it is from Him. So we don't need to be afraid of our boss and what he can do to us, because we are doing an excellent job for God and He will reward us.

What really blesses an employer is when you do more than he asked you to do, you do it according to the book, and you do it well. If you have a good boss, that will make him happy because it will make him look good for hiring you and training you. If he's not a good boss, he will get jealous and afraid that you will get his job. So then you sit down and tell him, "I'm not after your job, boss. I'm after getting you a promotion. I'm trying to make you look good."

He'll probably scratch his head and say, "What's your angle? What do you want out of this?"

You'll say, "Nothing. As a matter of fact, not a thing. I didn't come here for anything except to do a great job and bless you and the business."

Instead of embracing you, he might begin to talk evil about you. Why? He really loves all the work you do. He appreciates your great attitude. But what unnerves him is that you're not afraid of him or of losing your job. That's not why you're doing what you're doing. He is upset because he cannot control you by fear. You don't fear man; you only fear God.

I remember the day my boss said, "Listen, I'm gonna tell you what. I'm gonna give you so much work. I'm gonna bury you, man. Do you understand that? I'm gonna bury you."

I said, "Boss, I appreciate you, and I like you so much that you don't have enough work to bury me. Have a great day!"

Most people are looking to find out how little they can do and still get a paycheck. How little can they do and still fit into the crowd? You know something? Children of God are not here on earth to fit into a crowd. They are here to lead the crowd to Jesus. And when they're leading the crowd to Jesus, they aren't afraid of the crowd. The crowd can't control them because they're following Him.

What the Bible tells us is that when we submit ourselves to our bosses and do an excellent job for them, we are submitting ourselves to God. It's all for Him. I want the people who work with me to submit themselves to God and not just to me. You see, I may make a mistake and tell them that I want them to do something they know is wrong. I want them to come to me and say, "Brother, you know, the Word says this, which seems to conflict with what you've asked me to do. Can you show me if I've missed it?" Or, "Pastor, I might not see the whole picture like you do, but I was wondering if it might not be better to go this way instead of that way."

My reaction to that kind of person is, "Wow! Bless God! I sure appreciate you coming to me about this situation because that was something I didn't think about. Thanks for stopping me from making a mistake." When I have that kind of attitude, people who work for me are not going to be afraid of running things by me if they have questions. And when we do make the final decision, I'm going to be more confident about the outcome of it because I have looked at different points of view.

Looking at different points of view does not kill your faith! What kills your faith is not lining up those views with God's Word and seeking the Holy Spirit's guidance in the midst of making a decision. In the end I may tell the person who works for me that I still want them to do what they think is the wrong thing to do. But I'll do that because I fear God and not man. I'm satisfied that not only is the decision right with the Word, but it is also what the Holy Spirit is leading me to do. The Word and the Spirit always agree.

BACK TO THE GARDEN

Where did the fear of man originate? In the Garden, of course. Before the fall, Adam and Eve were one. When you talked to Adam you talked to Eve. When you talked to Eve you talked to Adam. They didn't have two separate identities or agendas. They were going the same direction with the same motivations and the same beliefs and understanding.

After the fall, however, Adam and Eve saw each other very differently. The saw each other naked and were afraid. They were afraid of God, they were afraid for their safety, and they were afraid of each other. They tried to cover up with fig leaves, but when God came looking for them they still hid. Their focus was no longer primarily on God but on each other, and all they saw were their inadequacies and faults.

They began the big cover-up. They covered themselves with pride. They covered themselves with self-centeredness. They covered themselves with arrogance. They covered themselves with a number of evil emotional reactions to one another like rejection, suspicion, anger, and unforgiveness. And that was the beginning of the fear of man. When they ceased to fear God, they feared each other.

The Good News is that through the blood and resurrection of Jesus Christ we can reverse this curse. When we fear God, we drive out all fear of man. Then the whole world can be pressuring us and disagreeing with us, but we will sit there with a smile on our faces, standing for what we believe.

FEAR OF THE FUTURE

I read a magazine article that said psychiatrists now consider being happy a psychological malfunction. To be a happy person, you have to be psychologically maladjusted. If you're happy, you are living in some kind of a fantasy world. For this kind of statement, I use a new biblical phrase, "This stinketh." Yes, this kind of thinking will put you in the grave like Lazarus and you will stinketh.

This article said that everybody's depressed because that's just the kind of world we live in. Everybody's beat up. Everybody's having a hard time. And everybody's complaining about it. You know how to get yourself depressed? Just complain. I'm serious! Spend some time complaining about everything you don't like in your life, and I promise you that you'll get depressed in no time at all.

One of the reasons people like to talk about their problems is because they believe that if they dwell on the problems that are just slightly depressing, they won't be afraid of what could really devastate them and take them out. Some people like problems. And the reason they like problems is because they think that if they're filled with problems, nothing else can go wrong. They don't have to deal with the fear of what may happen in the future because things are already messed up in the present.

Healthy people worry that they're going to get sick. Happily married people worry that their spouse will cheat on them and they'll have to divorce. Parents worry that their kids will grow up and rob convenience stores. Then their kids worry that their dog will run away and never be found. The whole society is afraid of the future.

Some people are afraid of what they might or might not do in the future. They imagine all kinds of strange happenings and see themselves doing the wrong thing, making a mess of their lives, hurting others, and being just plain stupid.

You are going to make mistakes, but thank God, you are who He says you are. If you don't know who He says you are, then pick up your Bible and find out. Why is this so important? When you know who God says you are, then you aren't afraid of the future. You know you will make mistakes, but you also know that He doesn't see you as a mistake-maker. Because of Jesus He sees you as His own son or daughter.

Do you know why so many people go to all of these self-help groups? It's because they don't know and fear God, or they do know God but they don't know who God says they are. They have absolutely no idea what God says about them in the Bible, but they will tell you they are Christians.

For I know the plans I have for you," says the LORD. "They are plans for good and not for disaster, to give you a future and a hope.

JEREMIAH 29:11

If you don't know who you are in Christ, find out! The Bible tells you who you are and that you have a great future in the Lord.

FEAR OF DEATH

Forasmuch then as the children are partakers of flesh and blood, he also himself likewise took part of the same; that through death he might destroy him that had the power of death, that is, the devil;

And deliver them who through fear of death were all their lifetime subject to bondage.

HEBREWS 2:14,15

A person who is afraid to die is consumed by all the ways they could die. Sickness. Accidents. Crime. Terrorism. If that is all they're thinking about, they are in bondage. They are not living their lives to the fullest.

I lived like that until I was born again. Then Jesus set me free from the obsession and fear of death to live my life to the fullest. Should the Lord tarry, I know that there is an appointed time for me to go, according to Hebrews 9:27; and the Bible promises I will be satisfied with long life in Psalm 91:16. I believe this in my heart and say it with my mouth that I will die an old man, and I am not afraid of dying because I'll just go to heaven to be with Jesus.

When I was a deliveryman, I had a tremendous opportunity to minister to people. As a matter of fact, I ministered to more people then than I do now. I shared with them about Jesus and they believed me because I had a brown uniform instead of a collar. When you become a minister people become very suspicious! Anyway, I was delivering a package, and when this woman came to the door, I could see right away that she was ravaged by fear. Her face wasn't just white as a ghost; she looked like a ghost.

She was in her robe, and she also looked like she hadn't slept for months. I said, "Ma'am, I'm a Christian. Could I pray with you for just a moment? Can I share with you what I believe will help you?"

She said, "I'm a Christian as well."

I said, "Well ma'am, then all the more reason for us to spend this time together." So I stayed with her for a while and listened to her sad story of how she was dying of lupus disease. She had just found out that she was entering the final stages of it. She'd ordered her casket. In her mind she was dead, and her body was quickly catching up.

Then I preached the Word to her. I talked to her about her adoption into God's family. I told her she was delivered out of the kingdom of darkness and into the kingdom of the Son of His love. I taught her that Jesus had redeemed her from family curses because her father and younger sister had died of lupus disease.

I said to her, "Ma'am, everything that belonged to Jesus now belongs to you. He has not given you the spirit of fear, but a Spirit of power, love, and a sound mind. He has not given you up, and it is not His will for you to die. It's His will for you to live. What is your will?"

She complained some more, and then I preached and taught her the Word some more. I told her that the Lord was on her side, that she didn't have to fear what man could ever do to her, that she didn't have to be afraid anymore. I told her what it says in Psalm 73:26, "My flesh and my heart faileth: but God is the strength of my heart, and my portion for ever."

Then she complained some more and I preached some more. And finally she looked at me and said, "Then bless God! I don't have to be sick!"

I said, "Are you ready to pray?"

Jesus nearly always preached and taught the truth before He prayed for the sick. We need to stop praying shotgun prayers, hoping to hit the devil with buckshots going everywhere. Instead, we need to get God's Word on the subject, the sword of the Spirit, and when we're built up in faith let the enemy have it right between the eyes.

The woman said, "Yeah, let's pray." We prayed and cast fear and sickness out of her life.

As I was leaving I asked, "Well, do you believe you're healed?"

She said, "I'm healed in the name of Jesus!"

Every day when I drove past her house this thought kept running through my mind: She's dead. You prayed for her and she died. She died and you're a big fake. You ruined the last days of her life with false hope.

One day, as I was delivering a package to a jewelry store, I noticed a pretty woman that walked by me. Before I got too far away I felt somebody grab my arm. Before I could do anything I realized it was the pretty woman I had just passed and she was saying, "You!"

I said, "Moi?"

She said again, "You! You're the healer!"

I laughed and said, "No, ma'am! I sure appreciate that, but I'm not. Jesus is the Healer. I just work for Him."

She said, "Don't you know me?"

I said, "No, ma'am. I'm sorry, but I don't remember you."

Then she said, "I had lupus disease!" At that I blurted out her name and her address. She cried, "God healed me!"

"Hey, that's pretty good!" I said, "Tell me about it!"

She said, "Right now, I'm working with the International Lupus Foundation. The Chinese people have been here. The Japanese people are looking at me. They have got me under a microscope. The problem is that the lupus is not just in recession. They can't tell that it was anywhere near me!"

I said, "Thank God!"

That beautiful woman heard God's Word, her faith rose up at hearing the truth, and she blasted fear of death out of her life to the point that her body was totally healed. Thank God, Jesus destroyed the devil so that we wouldn't have to fear death.

BRING GOLIATH DOWN!

Who's the Goliath in your life? A Goliath in your life is a giant worry. Is it your health? Is it your job? Is it your spouse? Is it your church? Is it your children? Is it you? Is it the economy? Is it the War on Terror?

"Well, you never know how the economy's gonna go. I don't wanna buy a new car because the economy could go bad." Well, it just might, but when the flood came to the earth, there were eight people that were saved in an ark. And you can either ride on top of the situation with God, or you can worry yourself into an emergency lifestyle and drown in fear.

Let me ask you a very important question. How much money does it take to survive? When Satan shows up, there isn't enough money to make it. The only thing that's going to see you through is faith in God and obeying His Word and His Spirit.

You probably have a Goliath or two you would prefer not to deal with, but the more you don't deal with it, the bigger that giant of worry gets. The more he corners you, the more you must go on the offense with him. If you're always on the offense with Goliath, you never have to go on the defense. You'll never have to back up. Whenever you take a step forward, don't you ever back up! You kill Goliath just like David did, with the rock of God's Word. Find out what God's will is and do not confer with flesh and blood.

Right after I was born again, I was driving a school bus. Everything was great. Jesus and I had an awesome relationship.

When I'd wake up in the morning, He'd say, "I've been waiting for you. I'm so happy you're awake. We can have fun today. We can talk. We can laugh. We can pray. We can just have a wonderful day!"

Then one day the Lord told me, "I want you to go back to the insurance company and tell them that you embezzled money from them."

I said, "Jesus, I love You, but I don't want to go to jail."

When I told Linda, she said, "Well Robb, even if you go to jail, I'll wait for you." That's my wife—Sister Faithful! Faithful and true. But I was afraid. Fear began to dominate my life. Finally I came to the place where I feared the Lord more than I feared prison. I told Him that I would rather be filled with joy in prison than to be out of prison but locked up in fear of man and disobedience to Him. Without Him, my life was worthless and hopeless.

I said to the Lord, "Now listen, don't You make me look bad because they're not looking for You. They're looking for me! And when I tell them that God told me to do this, they're not going to look to You; they're just going to think I'm crazy."

The second I made that decision in my life, I was free! Not only that, but the situation worked out in a miraculous way. I would never be doing what I am doing today if I had not made the decision to confront the lie I once lived and obey the Lord. I am not encouraging anyone to tell their past mistakes unless Jesus tells them to. This is something I knew Jesus told me to do. It took some time, but I paid the insurance company every dime that I owed them. The company was bewildered by my act, but willingly and graciously allowed me to reconcile my wrongdoing. Again, I did this in obedience to the Lord, and I believe I wouldn't be pastoring and serving God the way I am today if I had not obeyed Him.

The reason people have so much trouble is because they're spending so much time thinking how *not* to do what God told them to do. They think about how it probably won't work, it can't be real, or it's not their job. But our only job is to believe what He says and do what He says. That's how you kill your giant of fear in whatever situation you're facing.

> *Those who live in the shelter of the Most High will find rest in the shadow of the Almighty.*
>
> *This I declare of the LORD: He alone is my refuge, my place of safety; he is my God, and I am trusting him.*
>
> *For he will rescue you from every trap and protect you from the fatal plague.*
>
> *He will shield you with his wings. He will shelter you with his feathers. His faithful promises are your armor and protection.*
>
> *Do not be afraid of the terrors of the night, nor fear the dangers of the day,*
>
> *nor dread the plague that stalks in darkness, nor the disaster that strikes at midday.*
>
> *Though a thousand fall at your side, though ten thousand are dying around you, these evils will not touch you.*
>
> PSALM 91:1-7 NLT

The fear of God is your answer to fear's domination. Fear cannot get a stronghold in your life or hinder you in any way when you are dwelling in the presence of the Most High God.

2 0

Trust God

God is not a man, that he should lie; neither the son of man, that he should repent: hath he said, and shall he not do it? or hath he spoken, and shall he not make it good?

NUMBERS 23:19

The whole of the Scriptures revolves around this one verse. All of truth is centered on it. There is no other verse in the Bible that means more. This verse transcends all others because it says that God doesn't lie and His Word is true. He doesn't say one thing one day and another thing the next day. It says that what He speaks He does. When He says it, He means it.

God is not like human beings. He doesn't lie. He cannot lie. He will only tell you the truth; in fact, He can only tell you the truth because He's incapable of saying anything but the truth.

That by two immutable things, in which it was impossible for God to lie, we might have a strong consolation, who have fled for refuge to lay hold upon the hope set before us:

Which hope we have as an anchor of the soul, both sure and stedfast, and which entereth into that within the veil.

HEBREWS 6:18,19

In hope of eternal life, which God, that cannot lie, promised before the world began.

TITUS 1:2

Our hope in God is the anchor of our soul. Our hope in God dispels all worry. When our soul is anchored to the hope in God's Word, which is true because He cannot lie, then we will not worry. We will stand strong through any challenge or adversity.

To overcome worry forever, you have to know that the truth always remains the same. Circumstances change. Temporal facts evolve and change. And any problem in your life or in the world is only temporal. Everything is subject to change except God and His Word. His Word never changes because He never changes. Because Jesus is the Son of God, He never changes either.

> *Jesus Christ the same yesterday, and to day, and for ever.*
>
> HEBREWS 13:8

This is a great comfort to us as we go through life because everything around us is changing constantly. Some of the changes are good. We like getting a raise or promotion, getting married and having children, or buying a new house or car. These are the kinds of changes that we like. But there are a lot of other changes that we dread, that cause us great worry and fear. We worry about being laid off from our job, finding out our teenagers are on drugs or having sex, being unable to pay the bills and having to sell our house and move into an apartment, or getting a bad report from the doctor.

The Bible tells us not to be worried about anything. (See Phil. 4:6.) The reason we can live in this crazy world and not be worried about anything is because whatever changes come, God and His Word remain the same. If good things come, we rejoice. If bad things come, we can still rejoice because they are subject to change back to our good. God tells us that in His Word.

> *And we know that all things work together for good to them that love God, to them who are the called according to his purpose.*
>
> ROMANS 8:28

Not only does God work all things to our good, but whatever battles we must fight are controlled by God. The days of our battles are numbered by Him. When Jesus delivered the madman of Gadara from the legion of demons, they came out and this is what they said.

> And, behold, they cried out, saying, What have we to do with thee, Jesus, thou Son of God? art thou come hither to torment us before the time?
>
> MATTHEW 8:29 (ITALICS MINE)

Even demons know that God holds times and seasons in His hands. Every situation in your life has a time limit—when you are walking with God according to His Word. If you are rebellious or have turned away from Him, you may prolong a difficult situation. But when your heart is right toward Him, everything you face has a time limit.

How long do you have to resist the temptations and endure the trials in life that you face? As long as God has you there. It might be a day, it might be a week, it might be a month. Regardless of the time, you must remember that it's not forever. Knowing this helps you to not worry about your future because even your temptations and trials will only last as long as God allows. He knows how much you can take.

> Like as a father pitieth his children, so the LORD pitieth them that fear him.
> For he knoweth our frame; he remembereth that we are dust.
>
> PSALM 103:13,14

Consider how the man of Gadera, who was demon possessed, felt just before Jesus delivered him. By the time Jesus stood in front of him, this guy was having only moments of clear thinking. The demons had possessed him and were controlling him, but he still had a few moments when he could choose Jesus over the devil. He was completely tormented, but he could still choose Jesus. He recognized his appointed time and was set free.

Let me tell you something. Anytime you're right at the door of deliverance, you'll feel the greatest amount of pressure. When the dawn is about to break in your life, you'll think, *My God, I can't take another day. I can't.* In the morning, you'll wish it was night. And in the night, you'll wish it was morning. Everything you see causes you pain and adds to your worry. But it's only for an appointed time. Everything has an appointed time.

> *For the vision is yet for an appointed time, but at the end it shall speak, and not lie: though it tarry, wait for it; because it will surely come, it will not tarry.*
>
> HABAKKUK 2:3

Whatever you go through in life cannot stop what God has ordained to take place in your life. The vision for your life is destined to happen because it is for an appointed time.

> *For we are his workmanship, created in Christ Jesus unto good works, which God hath before ordained that we should walk in them.*
>
> EPHESIANS 2:10

Every work you are to accomplish has been ordained by God. He has set a path for you to walk in, and all you have to do is follow the leading of the Holy Spirit and God's Word.

When you know God can't lie, and then you read His incredible promises to save you and keep saving you, to protect you and provide for you, to give you a hope and a future, and after all that in this life to spend eternity with Him—it really shouldn't be that difficult to trust Him and *Give Up Worry Forever!*

Endnotes

1

What Is Worry?

[1] http://dictionary.reference.com/search?q=worrier

[2] *Webster's New World College Dictionary,* Third Edition, Victoria Neufeldt, Editor-in-Chief (New York: Macmillan, Inc., 1996), p. 62.

3

How Did Jesus Deal With Worry?

[1] *Webster's New World College Dictionary,* p. 495.

9

Attacking Panic Attacks

[1] James Strong, LL.D., S.T.D., *The New Strong's Exhaustive Concordance of the Bible,* "Hebrew and Chaldee Dictionary," (Nashville, TN: Thomas Nelson Publishers, 1984), #1101.

11

My Testimony: Freedom From Worry About the Past

[1] http://www.gracenotes.info/topics/enoch.html (article by Dr. Randell Redic)

14

Our Inheritance of Peace

[1] Spiros Zhodiates, *The Hebrew-Greek Key Study Bible,* (Chattanooga, TN: AMG Publishers, 1991) p. 879.

17

God Delivers Us From Worry

[1] *Webster's New World College Dictionary,* Third Edition, Victoria Neufeldt, Editor-in-Chief (New York: Macmillan, Inc., 1996), p. 365.

Prayer of Salvation

God loves you—no matter who you are, no matter what your past. God loves you so much that He gave His one and only begotten Son for you. The Bible tells us that "...whoever believes in him shall not perish but have eternal life" (John 3:16 NIV). Jesus laid down His life and rose again so that we could spend eternity with Him in heaven and experience His absolute best on earth. If you would like to receive Jesus into your life, say the following prayer out loud and mean it from your heart.

Heavenly Father, I come to You admitting that I am a sinner. Right now, I choose to turn away from sin, and I ask You to cleanse me of all unrighteousness. I believe that Your Son, Jesus, died on the cross to take away my sins. I also believe that He rose again from the dead so that I might be forgiven of my sins and made righteous through faith in Him. I call upon the name of Jesus Christ to be the Savior and Lord of my life. Jesus, I choose to follow You and ask that You fill me with the power of the Holy Spirit. I declare that right now I am a child of God. I am free from sin and full of the righteousness of God. I am saved in Jesus' name. Amen.

If you prayed this prayer to receive Jesus Christ as your Savior for the first time, please contact us on the Web at **www.harrisonhouse.com** to receive a free book.

Or you may write to us at:

Harrison House
P.O. Box 35035
Tulsa, Oklahoma 74153

About the Author

Author of more than fifteen compelling books, magazine articles, and countless audio and video resources, Dr. Robb Thompson is an exceptionally skilled relational and leadership strategist. He travels the globe, seeding it with vital truths that he has gleaned from over twenty years of experience in the arena of human resource management.

Robb has dedicated his life to teaching ministers, training business executives, and mentoring government leaders, including heads of State, cabinet ministers, and royalty. His pragmatic, dynamic, and down-to-earth principles on success are equipping thousands in their pursuit of excellence.

Dr. Robb Thompson also serves as Founder and President for the International College of Excellence, a fully accredited Christian university dedicated to maximizing personal potential and equipping tomorrow's leaders. His television program, "Winning in Life," is viewed by millions in the United States and around the world. Robb Thompson is the senior pastor of Family Harvest Church, one of America's most influential and productive churches. He has been happily married to his wife, Linda, for over thirty years. They live in the Chicagoland area.

To contact Pastor Robb Thompson
please write to:

Winning in Life Ministries
P.O. Box 558009
Chicago, IL 60655

Or you may contact him through the Web site at
www.winninginlife.com.

Please include your prayer requests
and comments when you write.

www.harrisonhouse.com

Fast. Easy. Convenient!

- ◆ New Book Information
- ◆ Look Inside the Book
- ◆ Press Releases
- ◆ Bestsellers

- ◆ Free E-News
- ◆ Author Biographies
- ◆ Upcoming Books
- ◆ Share Your Testimony

For the latest in book news and author information, please visit us on the Web at www.harrisonhouse.com. Get up-to-date pictures and details on all our powerful and life-changing products. Sign up for our e-mail newsletter, *Friends of the House,* and receive free monthly information on our authors and products including testimonials, author announcements, and more!

Harrison House—
Books That Bring Hope, Books That Bring Change

The Harrison House Vision

Proclaiming the truth and the power
Of the Gospel of Jesus Christ
With excellence;

Challenging Christians to
Live victoriously,
Grow spiritually,
Know God intimately.